A Picture Postcard History of New York's Elmira, Corning & Vicinity

by Alfred N. Weiner

...a visual trip into the past for

- Bath
- Corning
- Elmira
- Hammondsport
- Havana Glen
- Horseheads
- Keuka Lake
- Montour Falls
- Odessa
- Painted Post
- Savona
- Seneca Lake
- Watkins Glen

ALMAR PRESS
4105 Marietta Drive
Binghamton, N.Y. 13903

Library of Congress Cataloging-in-Publication Data

Weiner, Alfred N.
  A picture postcard history of New York's
Elmira, Corning, and vicinity.

  Bibliography: p.
  1. Elmira Region (N.Y.)—History—Pictorial
works. 2. Corning Region (N.Y.)—History
—Pictorial works. 3. Elmira Region (N.Y.)
—Description and travel—Views. 4. Corning
Region (N.Y.)—Description and travel—Views.
5. Postcards—New York (State)—Elmira Region.
6. Postcards—New York (State)—Corning Region.
I. Title.
F129.E6W45   1988   974.7′78   88-941
ISBN 0-9350256-17-4

First Edition, First Printing: July 1988
Second Printing: December 1988

Cover design by Lee Stella
Design and Composition by Eastern Graphics, Binghamton, NY

Printed in the United States of America

For additional copies of this book or a copy of our latest catalog, write to:

ALMAR PRESS, 4105 Marietta Drive, Binghamton, N.Y. 13903

CONTENTS

DEDICATIONS

To Marilyn, who always provides the
enthusiastic encouragement and help.

To Bob, Carolyn, Dianna, and Linda for
their support and eagerness to assist
in whatever needs to be done.

PREFACE

Any attempt to write a detailed history of the cities and towns included in this book would require many volumes. Although these pages contain a history of the areas involved, it is not an academic study. Rather, it is a particular approach to the representation of each locality from the snapshot or still picture viewpoint.

The postcard (or View as it is known to postcard collectors) is a snapshot in time. It represents a building, street, home, scenic wonder, specific event, or any other subject involving human endeavor at the moment the picture was taken. Many of the views can be combined as a series of photographs taken of the same scene over a period of years to form a history of the scene. This combination was used for some of the streets shown in this book.

The postcard was initially used as an inexpensive and rapid means of communication between people. It provided space for a short written message and a photograph of a scene—often in color—that was significant to the writer.

The communication written on the postcard may or may not have been related to the scene. For example, the writer may have used a postcard showing a photograph of an important building in the town to inquire about the health of the recipient.

Many of these postcards were collected for the message, history, and the photographic scene. Today, as a result of these collecting interests we have a very valuable source of information from an historical prespective. The postcards show us the status of a community during specific time periods in the past.

Any collection of these postcards representing the history of a city, town, and area must be incomplete by the nature of the availability and selection of the views. Fortunately, people collected these views and they were passed on in time to other members of their family and friends. However, all buildings, streets, and scenic wonders were not recorded on postcards and all of the available postcards were not saved.

As a result, this book represents a careful collection and selection of the available views representing the specified localities. In some instances only one postcard was available to this writer; although, I am certain that other views must exist.

The descriptive captions for each view offer historical information combined with the comments of many interested people (see ACKNOWLEDGEMENTS TO THE MANY HELPERS) and this writer. No claim is made to originality or completeness in the captions.

For the reader's interest, the arrangement of the postcards represents an automobile trip West from Binghamton, New York to the Elmira and Corning area along the scenic highway, N.Y. Route 17. Within each of the cities and towns, the views are arranged as a walking tour through the community.

A note to the Deltioligists:

To provide reference information for your collection of these views, the following information was taken from each view and added it to the end of each caption.

Publisher: (Card No. and the name and address of the publisher)
Manufacturer: (Name and address)

If any of these items of information are not printed on either side of the view then "Not Indicated" is shown below the caption. There are captions that show all three items, some show one or more items, and some show none of the items.

ACKNOWLEDGEMENTS TO THE MANY HELPERS.

This book is the result of help from many interested people. Most of the contents—information and postcards (views)—were provided by many helpful and considerate people willing to contribute their time, knowledge, and postcards to the completion of this book.

The following listing is a brief description of the assistance that was provided. The names are not listed in any specific sequence except as my initial contact with the person relative to the development of this book.

I am grateful for the valuable advice offered by Harvey N. Roehl, The Vestal Press Limited, who originated the concept of showing views with captions in this book format. His willingness to always provide constructive help assured completion of this book.

Thomas P. Dimitroff provided most of the views of Corning for reproduction and important information to help describe the scenes. His book (coauthered with Louis S. Janes) HISTORY OF THE CORNING PAINTED POST AREA: 200 YEARS IN PAINTED POST COUNTRY was a constant source of reference in preparing the text. His critical review of the manuscript pertaining to Corning was very helpful in eliminating errors. He also placed the views in a logical order as a tour through Corning and the surrounding area.

Thomas E. Byrne provided an important critical review of the manuscript relating to the Elmira area. His book, CHEMUNG COUNTY 1890-1975 was used as a primary reference for information pertaining to the Elmira Area. He provided many helpful comments for the preparation of the Elmira portion of the book.

Janet H. Howell provided excellent research information describing the Elmira-Corning Area. The information she obtained became the basis for many parts of the text.

Barbara Bell provided the views of Watkins Glen and the surrounding area for reproduction. She developed the significant information that was used to describe the scenes shown on the views.

Sheldon S. King offered valuable information pertaining to the publication and manufacture of many of the views shown in this book.

Grandison Gridley, Dave Collins, Sr., Alfred (Chick) Hilbert, and Robert Richter generously offered views from their collections for selection and use in this book.

Richard A. Friend for his information helping to describe the Elmira views and his work in placing the views in a logical order as a tour through Elmira.

Richard G. Sherer for providing valuable information relating to Bath and Hammondsport.

Lorri Lanmon for providing information pertaining to Mark Twain at Quarry Farm.

Many important items of information used in this book were based on discussions with the people in the Research Dept. of the Vestal Public Library and the Research Dept. of the Boome County Public Library.

I have made a careful effort not to omit any person who provided help in the preparation of this book. If an omission has occured please advise me for proper acknowledgement to be included in the next printing of this book.

My "Thank You" goes to everyone involved. This book would not have been completed without all of this help.

Alfred N. Weiner
Binghamton, New York
February 1988

INTRODUCTION

CONGRESSMAN AMO. HOUGHTON . . .

Once a long time ago a friend of mine suggested that we might all be better off if we were to seek out a desert island belonging to no nation which, with no discernible history, would then free us to do what we wanted—provide a springboard for a free and happy life.

But, you see I was one up on my friend. I had read and dreamt along with Walter D. Edwards in *Drums Along the Mohawk*. I had camped on Spencer Hill, walked in Herkimer County, driven through the Cherry Valley, and glided effortlessly in a sail plane over the grand old Indian villages of Horseheads and Big Flats in Upstate New York.

Corning has been my base since the early morning of August 7, 1926. Now, there are hundreds, maybe thousands of Cornings in this country. But, as you can well imagine this particular Corning is special. The geography is O.K., the weather is passable. It's the atmosphere, the history, the surrounding countryside, the people, the way of life—that makes it special.

And what memories—trout fishing on a late July afternoon at Castle Creek near Avoca; sliding and tumbling in the altogether down the moss-covered rocks into the mountain cool pools at Glenora; watching a German system shop blow a beautiful glass cylinder in "A" factory; praying in the breathtakingly beautiful Garret Chapel on the bluff at Keuka Lake; gazing at Seneca Lake in the walkway of the old Glen Springs Hotel; climbing on the Mohican statue at Painted Post; racing my brothers and sisters for the water hole above the bridge in Savona.

Odessa, Havana Glen, Moutour Falls, Hammondsport—this is "Upstate"—a part of New York that is hard not to like. It's a place where pockets of new science, new machinery, new services and ideas walk hand in hand with the old, the stable, the decent.

If I were just starting out, I'd move here in a second. It's the ideal spot for the dual career couple—a place to work, to live, but most importantly to bring up your children. When everything one has strived for in life is tallied, the one essential element is your children. While we work, and carry water on both shoulders in the high energy years, in the back of our minds is the ever present question: Do our children live and breathe the right atmosphere, have the elbow room, see the right standards set, learn to have confidence in themselves?

If not in whole, certainly in part the answer could easily be, yes—if one were able to take advantage of that special piece of real estate-"Upstate."

This is why what this book represents is so important to those of us who feel a particular allegiance to our unique part of this country.

HISTORIAN THOMAS E. BYRNE . . .

Postcards have a way of mirroring the business and social history of a community. Long before the days of the Instamatic and the Polaroid, the ubiquitous postcard photographer was snapping away at downtown Elmira. These postcards of the 1890-1940 period reflect the life and times of the Queen City. And they review many institutions vital to Chemung County's advance.

INTRODUCTION

HISTORIAN THOMAS P. DIMITROFF . . .

Deltiology, the collecting and study of postcards, is one of the fastest growing recreational and investment hobbies in America today. Its appeal reaches out to young and old alike. Additionally, postcards are sought after and pondered over by scholars and journalists. All of this is of no surprise to collectors and enthusiasts who have already availed themselves of the wealth of information, humor, joy, and understanding presented through these unique artifacts. Postcards are unique for they are not only evidences and reflections of the times and cultures that produced them, but are also vital statements about the values and priorities of the people who produced, purchased, and used them.

Like the history they are a part of, postcards can be categorized chronologically. The true "antique" postcards were produced from about 1893 until 1915. Postcards during this era showed almost all elements of a community and a community's life. They were also used as holiday greeting cards. This was a slower era, a time when many took the time to write their thoughts to others who they knew would take the time to read them. Postcards then were as personal as a phone call or a visit. This was a time of great change seeing America transform itself from a predominately agrarian, rural society to a highly industrial one with great and growing cities. Americans were changing their nations by developing an amazing railroad system, adopting the automobile and saying hello to the airplane. They also electrified their streets, homes, and vactories, wove and web of telephone lines across the country, and, in general, settled down to the business of becoming "modern."

The period which followed, from about 1915 to the 1930's, also was exciting and saw growth continue and America become truly international by plunging into a World War. We also adopted Prohibition, survived the "Roaring Twenties," and gave the vote to women. Then, the greatest economic disaster in our history, the Great Depression" descended like a cloak of darkness over the nation. Through it all, postcards, now of the "white border" type, continued to picture our communities, their people, and their activities.

"Linen" postcards replaced the earlier "white borders" for much of the 1930's and 1940's. World War II occupied most people's attention during much of this period, but the prosperity that followed soon was reflected in cards from communities all over the United States. Since the 1950's postcards have been called "chromes" and picture communities in glossy, professional, and rather commercial ways. They seem to have lost much of both the role and nature of earlier cards.

In a collective way, all postcards from all eras give us a picture of America through its people and its communities. A great deal of American History is there. We can catch glimpses of picnics, parades, weddings, funerals, sporting events, buildings, bridges, streets, cars, trains, ships, and much, much more. We can see the triumphs and follies of our ancestors and their friends and neighbors. Most of all we can see a panorama of the changes of a nation, and we can see it as reflected through our neighborhoods and communities. This brings American History into focus.

This book helps us view this panorama for it is about both postcards and our local communities. Above all else it is enjoyable. It presents us with a visual trip into the past that allows us to peek into the communities of this part of the Allegheny Plateau. When we peek, we perceive both similarities and differences. As we wander through the pictures and words, we begin to further enjoy our glimpses into yesteryears for they are enhanced by being views through the eyes of those that lived them. This book is something very different from a definitive history of either the Southern Tier of New York State or any of its individual communities. Its purpose is to welcome readers to the exciting and wonderful experience of discovering more about themselves, their neighbors, their communities, and their world through the magic of the picture postcard.

ELMIRA, N. Y. SULLIVAN MONUMENT.

This field stone monument was dedicated to General Sullivan on August 29, 1879 at what is now called the Newtown Battlefield State Park. Generals Sullivan and McClellan were present to honor the victory that avenged the massacres of Wyoming and Cherry Valley. General George Washington had ordered General Sullivan to clear the area of the Indians. He began in Easton, PA., with 3500 men and reached Tioga Point (Athens) for the battle of Newtown on August 29, 1779. Newtown was regarded as an important battle of the Revolutionary War as it opened Upstate New York for the new nation. The present marble monument that replaced the crumbling field stone was dedicated on August 29, 1912.

Publisher: Card No. E7816, C. S. Woolworth & Company, Elmira, NY.
Manufacturer: Made in Germany.

Publisher: Not indicated.
Manufacturer: Not indicated.

1

Newtown Creek at foot of E. Water St., Elmira, N.Y.

This photograph shows the point where Newtown Creek flows into the Chemung River. The Village of Newtown was initially designed by Mr. Jeffery Wisner. The first buildings were erected in 1790 on what became Sullivan Street. There were log cabins and a courthouse. A legislative act in 1811 changed the name of Newtown to Elmira.

Publisher: Not Indicated.
Manufacturer: Not Indicated.

ARNOT MILL DAM, ELMIRA, N.Y.   221662

Mr. Stephen Tuttle came to Newtown (Elmira) in 1818. Together with Mr. Guy Maxwell he built the Tuttle Mills near the mouth of the Newtown Creek. The mills later became known as the Arnot Mills. Mr. Tuttle owned all of the land between the mill and the city and later donated much of the land to the city.

Publisher: Card No. 221662, Not Indicated.
Manufacturer: Metropolitan Company, Everett, MA.

This view of West Water Street shows the new Elevated Railroad that was operational in 1934. The following businesses were established at these addresses:

105–111—Merchants Bank

106—Richman Brothers Clothing

108—Park Lane Shoe Store

110—Allyn's Young Folks Shop

112—Rosenbaum's

114–116—Walsh & Regan Furniture

115–119—Kobackers Furniture

118–120—S.S. Kresge Variety

121—Chic Millinary

122–124—F. W. Woolworth

123—Ormond Hosiery Shop

125—Union Store Inc.

126–128—J. J. Newberry

127—Eckerd's Cut Rate Store

130–132—W. T. Grant

WEST WATER ST., ELMIRA, N. Y., SHOWING NEW ELEVATED RAILROAD.

Apparently, parking was also a problem in Downtown Elmira during this time; note the bumper-to-bumper line of automobiles parked on both sides of the street.

Publisher: Rubin Bros., Elmira, NY.
Manufacturer: Metropolitan, Everett, MA.

9053. The Hulett Building, Elmira, N. Y.

The Hulett Building was built circa 1910 by Mrs. Harriet Arnot Rathbone and owned by the Arnot Realty Co. It was located on the Southwest corner of Lake and Water Streets. The building was razed after the 1972 flood. The first two floors were occupied by the Elmira Water and Railroad Co. in 1900. Then the Elmira Light and Heat & Power Co. in 1932, and the New York State Electric & Gas Co. in 1936. The other floors contained a variety of business offices during those years.

Publisher: Card No. 9053, Acmegraph Company, Chicago, IL.
Manufacturer: Not Indicated.

Street Scene, Main St. at Water St., Elmira, N. Y.

100–108 Elenor K. Footwear Co.

101–107—A. F. Werdenberg Co.

102—Murphy's Haberdasher

108—Karmelkorn Shop

109—Thrifty Day Cleaners

110—Franklin Crayton

111–115—J. C. Penney (Snyder Bldg.)

112—George Knietsch Bookstore & Lester Gamble Optician

114—Hudson Shoe Co.

117—Elmira Arms

118—Wright Electric Co.

A view from the corner at Main and Water Streets taken in 1932. The Gorton Coy Building at the right corner was completed in that year. The trolley tracks in the foreground lead from the Main Street Bridge. The following businesses were established at these addresses:

Publisher: Card No. 35469, Rubin Bros., Elmira, NY.
Manufacturer: Metropolitan, Everett, MA.

119—Buell Floral Co.

120—Federal Bake Shop & Simon P. Sheridan Tailor

121–125—Schweppe Bldg.

123—Colonial Theater

129—French Shop Ladies Wear

131–133 Edgecomb's Furniture

134—F. W. Woolworth Co.

135—Bedrosians Bros.

139—Montgomery Ward

144—John W. Robertson & Van Nort Pharmacy

150—S. F. Iszard and Co.

156—Mark Twain Hotel

Elmira N.Y., The Dininny Residence, West Water Street

Mr. Ferral Dininny was born in Otego County on January 22, 1818. He was a succesful lawyer and elected to the State Assembly in 1852. In 1860, he gave up most of his law practice and joined Mr. John Arnot and others in Elmira to form the Blossburg Coal Co. Between 1872 and 1876, he built a home on West Water Street described as the "Finest and most costly in Elmira." Included in the home was an art gallery, porte cochere on the east side, pillars, porch, and windows with hand-carved trim. The interior included ceiling high mirrors in the hall, Waterford Chandeliers, a huge walnut staircase, walnut panel dining room, and a drawing room hung with gold-colored velvet. The red brick carriage house faced Gray Street. After Mr. Dininny died in 1901, the home was opened to the public. The home was razed in 1910.

Publisher: Card No. 4459, Hugh C. Leighton Company, Portland, ME.
Manufacturer: Frankfort, Germany.

Main Street, Elmira, N. Y.

15075

Publisher: Card No. 15075, Rubin Bros., Elmira, NY.
Manufacturer: Metropolitan, Everett, MA.

The Traffic Control Tower was in use at Main Street and Water Street in the 1920's. The following businesses were established at these addresses:

101–107—A. F. Werdenberg Co. Men's Clothing

111–115—Snyder Bldg.

11—Grand Union Tea Co.

113—Claude Buckpitt, Music

115—The Chocolate Shop

Car for Rorick's Glen-Corner Main & Water St. Elmira, N.Y.

The trolley car ride to Rorick Glen was always the signal that a good time was in store for all involved. The ride began in a busy part of the city. The store on the left in the photograph is Werdenberg's Inc., founded in 1898 by Mr. Andrew F. Werdenberg with a partner, Mr. Milton Cisco. In 1903, Mr. A. D. Merrill and Mr. Arthur Burt joined the company. The company continues in operation at the Northwest Corner of Water and Main Streets. The building on the opposite (Northeast) Corner was occupied by Mr. Thomas Routledge, Jeweler; it was replaced in 1932 by the Gorton Coy Building. The company began in 1916 when Mr. Warren A. Gorton of Batavia purchased The Fashion Shop of Mr. E. N. Crandall. The store closed in the 1970's. This corner was the location of the Tavern House (Franklin House). Later it was known as the Higgins Block and the Padgett Block.

The trolley car of the Elmira Water Light and Railway Company was called the "Setback" and it ran from the Roricks Glen Loop to the end of the line at Clark's Glen. In this three-car arrangement, the powered trolley car pulled the two powerless former horse-drawn cars.

Publisher: Not Indicated.
Manufacturer: Not Indicated.

East Water Street had the following businesses established at these addresses in 1928:

101–103—F & W Grand
    Stores

105—Central Pharmacy

107—Logan's Ready To
    Wear

109—Regent Theater

111—Fanny Farmer Candy

113—The Great A & P Tea
    Company

115–117—J.P. & M.
    Sullivan Furniture

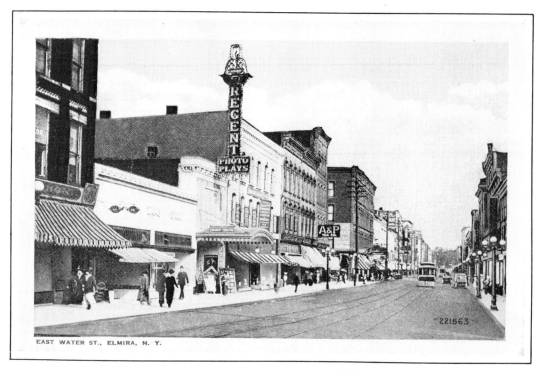

EAST WATER ST., ELMIRA, N. Y.

Publisher: Card No. 221563, Rubin Bros., Elmira, NY.
Manufacturer: Not Indicated.

EAST WATER STREET FROM RAILROAD AVENUE, ELMIRA, N. Y.

This photograph, taken circa 1925, is looking at East Water Street from Railroad Avenue. The following businesses were established at these addresses:

109—Regent Theater (Note the upper portion of the "Regents
    Photo Plays" sign had been removed when this photograph
    was taken.)

111–113—Hallock Bros. Clothiers

115—J. P. & M. Sullivan Furniture

117—Laskaris & Son Ice Cream & Confection
Corner of Water And State Streets—Canal Trust Co.

Publisher: Card No. 106446, Rubin Bros., Elmira, NY.
Manufacturer: Tichnor Bros., Boston, MA.

Lake Street from Water Street,
Elmira, N. Y.

Looking up Lake Street from Water Street in 1913, the following businesses were established at these addresses:

Corner—Charles D. Metzger Restaurant & Saloon

100–112—Elmira Advertiser

104—Flynn's Cigar Store

106—Enright & Lazarus Saloon

109–113—Barker, Rose, & Clinton Hardware

115–117—Queen City Hotel

119—William F. Maurer Saloon & Restaurant

Note the man standing at the center of the photograph, with his back to the camera is a Policeman intent on directing traffic and the man to his right side, standing on the streetcar tracks is wearing a *"Transit Authority"* uniform.

Publisher: Not Indicated
Manufacturer: Curteich Company, Chicago, IL.

During the first three years of the Civil War, Elmira had a military depot consisting of four assembly areas. In early 1864, Barracks No. 3 located on West Water Street was empty and the government decided to convert it into a Confederate Prison Camp. This unit contained 35 wooden buildings, each 110 feet long and 16 feet wide; with sufficient height to be suitable for two vertical rows of bunks. A fence 12 feet high was built around the entire area. The barracks would hold 4000 prisoners and tents could be placed in the available space for an additional 1000 prisoners. On July 6, 1864, 400 young and old men arrived and by the end of August there were 9,618 prisoners. Of the total of 12,123 men, 2,963 died and were buried at Woodlawn Cemetery.

Publisher: Not Indicated.
Manufacturer: Not Indicated.

9046. The Dam in the Chemung, Elmira, N. Y.

On January 27, 1824, the legislature authorized the erection of a dam across the Chemung River. Many opponents to the dam thought it would obstruct navigation; however, the need for flour and wooden boards and the water power required to produce these products provided the approval for the dam. Initially, authority was given to Mr. Isaac Baldwin to build the dam near the Lake Street Bridge. Public disapproval of this location required a change to the foot of College Avenue —originally named Mill Street. The dam was named the Baldwin Dam and in 1927 the name was changed to the Record Dam.

Publisher: Card No. 9046, Not Indicated.
Manufacturer: Acmegraph, Chicago, IL.

At the death of Dr. Thomas K. Beecher, the congregation of the Park Church and the people of Elmira wished to provide a memorial in his honor. Funds were collected for the Beecher Monument which is located in Wisner Park. The statue is by Mr. Jonathan Scott Hartley, a sculptor known for his keen analysis of character and for the technical excellence of his work. Dr. Beecher did not refer to himself as a minister of the gospel, he described himself as a "Teacher of The Park Church". His doctrine was the Fatherhood of God and the Brotherhood of Man. He walked around Elmira in ordinary clothes and considered himself a man of work and play. The minister was the son of Mr. Lyman Beecher, eminent theologian, preacher, and reformer. The siblings of Dr. Thomas Beecher were distinguished in their own efforts, notably, Mr. Henry Ward Beecher and Mrs. Harriet Beecher Stowe, author of Uncle Tom's Cabin.

Publisher: Souvenir Post Card Company, New York, NY.
Manufacturer: Not Indicated.

7676—Beecher Monument. Elmira, N. Y.

Dear friend, I am having a fine time wish you were here I have been to Sullivan Beach wish you would

WISNER PARK, SHOWING BEECHER MONUMENT, ELMIRA, N.Y. PARK CHURCH IN BACKGROUND.

Wisner Park located at Main and Church Streets was Wisner Cemetery and Baptist Cemetery. The land was deeded by Mr. Jeffery Wisner, son of Mr. Henry Wisner an early landowner of the Village of Newtown. (Newtown was the name of Elmira before 1811.) In 1858, all of the people buried in Wisner Cemetery were moved to Woodlawn Cemetery and the empty land became Wisner Park. The statue of Dr. Thomas K. Beecher faces Main Street with Park Church behind him.

Publisher: Card No. A-52425, Rubin Bros., Elmira, NY.
Manufacturer: Curteich, Chicago, !L.

The Helen L. Bullock Industrial Training School For Girls, known as the *"Anchorage"* was a training school for wayward girls, located at 955 College Avenue. The 40 girls who could occupy the home each had their own room. Donations were accepted for food, bedding, clothing, and anything suitable for the home. Mrs. Bullock stated the purpose of the training school was to welcome: *"The tempted, homeless, and friendless girl to a better environment . . . to offer a helping hand which could save them from a life of sin, to turn the current of their lives into a channel of purity and usefulness and independence instead of leaving them to become criminals and paupers, thus leading many others down with them."* The girls between the ages of 12 to 18 years maintained the following regime:

The Helen L. Bullock, Industrial Training School for Girls, ELMIRA, N. Y.

Publisher: Not indicated.
Manufacturer: Not Indicated.

5:30AM	Wake up	12:00	Dinner	7:00–8:00	Study
6:30	Breakfast followed by morning prayers. Morning duties in laundry or kitchen.	2:00PM	School	8:30	Worship
		4:00	Recreation	9:00	Bedtime
		5:30	Supper		

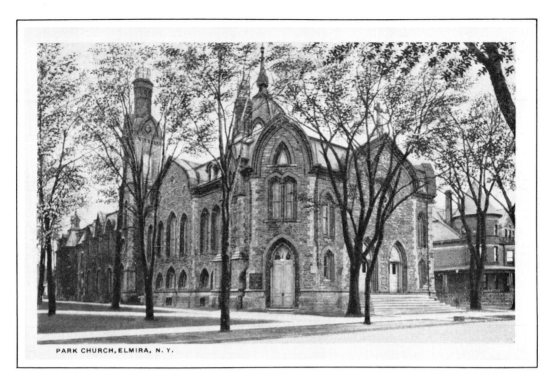

PARK CHURCH, ELMIRA, N.Y.

The Park Church, at the corner of Main and Church Streets, was built as the result of a decision made on January 3, 1871 by the founders to build a new facility. Dr. Thomas K. Beecher was the minister and he continued in that position until his death in 1900. The plan for the building, considered revolutionary for the 1870 period, provided an auditorium with accomodations for 800 seated adults and an additional 200 to 300 adults in a gallery. An important feature was a free public library.

The kitchen was equipped with china and silver for 200 to 300 people. The parlors were available to anyone who wished to use them. Pool and billard tables, a dance hall, a children's play room, and a theater were all included for use in 1873. During the 1950s, the chimneys were removed and the plain glass windows were replaced by stained glass windows.

Publisher: Not Indicated.
Manufacturer: Not Indicated.

First Baptist Church, Elmira, N.Y.

The First Baptist Church, on Church Street, was built in 1892 at a cost of $70,000. The design by Dockstader and Pierce includes an enormous sanctuary, parlors, offices, gymnasium, kitchens, and a library. The building contains a variety of building materials including brick, terra cotta, tile, and stone in the Queen Anne style of construction. The tower, a landmark of the era, is shaped as a lantern in the Christian symbol of light. The stained glass windows do not tell a story in the traditional sense; they include a display of flowers and birds reflecting an arts and crafts consideration.

Publisher: Not Indicated.
Manufacturer: Not Indicated.

The site for construction of The Armory was approved on July 3, 1886 by Major General Josiah Porter, Adjutant General of the New York National Guard. The land was purchased for $10,000 from the John Arnot, Sr. estate. Construction of the three-story brick building began in 1886. It cost $23,487. Over the years, improvements to the building included an electric elevator for aging Civil War Veterans, bowling alleys, and nuclear fallout shelters. The Armory was abandoned in 1985.

THE ARMORY, E. CHURCH ST., ELMIRA, N. Y.

Publisher: Card No. 25520, Elmira Tobacco Company, Elmira, NY.
Manufacturer: Dexter Press, Pearl River, NY.

"HOTEL RATHBURN," ELMIRA, N. Y.

The Chemung Canal, the railroads, and the Civil War helped to make hotels a necessity in Elmira. The Hotel Rathburn was known originally as The Brainard. Built by Mr. John T. Brainard, it was opened for the completion of the Erie Railroad in 1851. When Mr. Brainard died, his wife sold it to Mr. John T. Rathburn. The hotel was razed in 1941.

Located at the corner of Baldwin and Water Streets, the hotel was described in the Centennial issue of The Star Gazette, by Mr. W. Charles Barber: *"Of all the hotels Elmira ever had, the one with the longest life, and the greatest reknown was the Rathbun at Water and Baldwin Streets. The hotel, a tall commodious brick structure much like New York's Murray Hill Hotel, was famous for the table it set . . ."*

Publisher: Card No. 39447, Rubin Bros., Elmira, NY.
Manufacturer: Not Indicated.

A project that lighted the way to Chemung County's current United Community Services was initiated by a group of prominent Elmira Women in 1905. They were ahead of their time, in seeking to consolidate the various city charitable organizations. Institutions of the time were the industrial School, The Orphans' Home, The Home For The Aged, The Anchorage, The Sunshine Circles, and The Visiting Nurse Association.

A $60,000 structure was planned and Mr. J. Sloat Fassett donated the site at the Northeast Corner of Church and State Streets. His wife, Mrs. Jennie Crocker Fassett gave $15,000 to the building Fund. When the Womens

Federation Building, as shown in the photograph, opened in 1908, the objective was to halt the overlapping relief work and to supply *"Such material help as will put them (the needy) on their feet and make them self-supporting."* The ground floor was for industrial school purposes, laundry, sewing, cooking, the Omega Club Training School, and a swimming pool. The second floor had offices, cafeteria, kitchen, and a hall with seats for 900. The third floor was for agencies, the fourth floor had a gym and a few sleeping rooms. The roof included a garden and nursery.

The Elmira Federation For Social Service of 1912 later became the Community Chest-Red Cross Organization, and finally the United Way. The building was razed in the 1970s and the new Steele Library now occupies the site.

Publisher: Card No. C-23, Baker Bros., Elmira, NY.
Manufacturer: Not Indicated.

The red brick mansion with the classical facade and Ionic columns shown in the photograph is the Arnot Art Museum on Lake Street. The home was built by Mr. John Arnot in the 1830's. When Mr. Matthias H. Arnot died in 1910 there was an estate of $2.16 Million and his art treasures. The art treasures were left to the public, housed in a private gallery in the North wing of the home. The Arnot Art Gallery opened to the public in 1913 with Mrs. Eugene M. Diven as Director. A large portion of the collection was purchased from the estate of Lord Hamilton of England in 1882. The will provided for: *"The establishment of a Gallery Corporation to which be bequeathed the buildings and grounds."* Mr. Arnot's expressed wish was, *"To establish, maintain, and add a gallery and museum of objects of educational, artistic, historic, or literary character and value: with free access to the public and to encourage and develop the study of the fine arts and kindred subjects, and advance the general knowledge thereof."*

Publisher: Card No. 12887, Not Indicated.
Manufacturer: Metropolitan Company, Everett, MA.

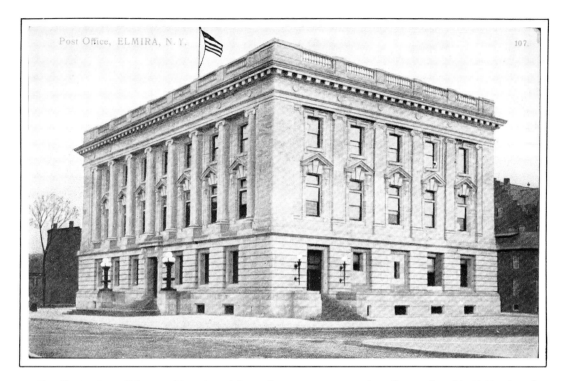

The Elmira Post Office at Church and State Streets was opened on September 13, 1903 when Postmaster David M. Pratt raised the American Flag on the building. The Post Office was transferred from the Masonic Temple on Lake Street during that day. The people of Elmira were impressed by the lobby walls made of Vermont Marble, the oak woodwork, and marble staircase, all built at a cost of $275,000. The current Elmira Post Office is located across the street and to the west of the the original building shown in the photograph. This building is now owned by the Aetna Life Insurance Co.

Publisher: Not Indicated.
Manufacturer: Not Indicated.

THE CENTURY CLUB, ELMIRA, N. Y.

The Century Club was organized in Elmira, in 1880, to provide for *"Social intercourse among the professional and business men."* Mr. Alexander S. Divan was the first President. The initial quarters for the club were in the Masonic Temple, then from 1899 to 1906 in the Robinson Building. Billiards, pool, and whist were popular activities. The club was a frequent host to Mr. Samuel Clemens. The bylaws prohibited drinking of intoxicating liquor, and *"playing for stake, bet, or wager."* In 1906, with a membership of 600, the club moved into the building shown in the photograph at 214 East Church Street. There were bowling alleys in the base- ment, lunch service upstairs, and card parties for the wives of members. This large and influential social club faded away during the Depression years. In 1933, the building was sold to the Knights of Columbus and today it is owned by the Yunis Realty.

Publisher: Not Indicated.
Manufacturer: Not Indicated.

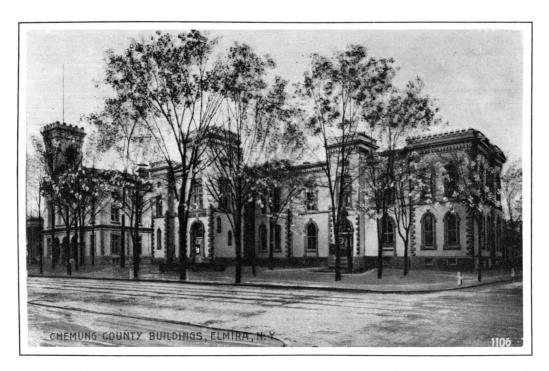

CHEMUNG COUNTY BUILDINGS, ELMIRA, N.Y.

Elmira, as the County Seat for Chemung County, required a courthouse. The building at the left in the photograph was designed by Mr. Horatio Nelson White and erected in 1862. The Board of Supervisors pronounced it an architectural beauty of convenience and durability. A new County Clerk's Building was built behind the Courthouse. It was completed in 1875 at a cost of $21,890.25. An annex at the right (East) end of the Clerk's office was completed in 1894 as a County Jail. It had 24 cells and two dungeons to hold unmanageable prisoners. The building cost $59,926 and included quarters for the Sheriff and a Children's Shelter.

Publisher: Card No. 1106, Not Indicated.
Manufacturer: Not indicated.

City Hall, Elmira, N. Y.

Elmira's City Hall was located on Market Street in 1890, the current site of the Elks Club. The existing City Hall, shown in the photograph, was built in 1896 for $118,000. It was considered a beautiful structure designed by Elmira Architects Pierce and Bickford. The elaborate capitals supported by ornamental columns was a style taken from the World Columbian Exposition in Chicago, Illinois. The South and East pediments are decorated with terra cotta figures representing agriculture, arts, and science. A fire on November 18, 1909 damaged City Hall. The pediments were unscathed and despite the fact that the clock and roof fell into ruin, $30,000 was spent to rehabilitate City Hall. The building remains essentially the same today with the addition of a two-story fire escape and access for the handicapped.

Publisher: Card No. 35467, Not Indicated.
Manufacturer: Not Indicated.

Elmira needed a new hotel in the late 1920's. During February 1928, a referendum on the question of the city widening Gray Street for the hotel site was defeated. The hotel developer, Mr. J. John Hassett offered a 17 x 170 foot strip of his land as a gift to the city provided Gray Street was widened. Mr. Hassett also purchased $300,000 of the Million Dollar Bond issue. Mr. Frederic H. Hill and Mr. Arthur B. McLeod were also involved in the purchase of the bonds. The Mark Twain Hotel opened on March 23, 1929 with a gala event. A banquet for the Committee of One Hundred for the selling of $300,000 of the bonds was held. The hotel was built by the Lowman Construction Co. and Mr. L. H. Vanderslice was the first manager. The Mark Twain is now an apartment hotel.

Mark Twain Hotel at Elmira, N. Y. — D-13

Publisher: Card No. D-13, Queen City Paper Company, Elmira, NY.
Manufacturer: Dexter Press, Pearl River, NY.

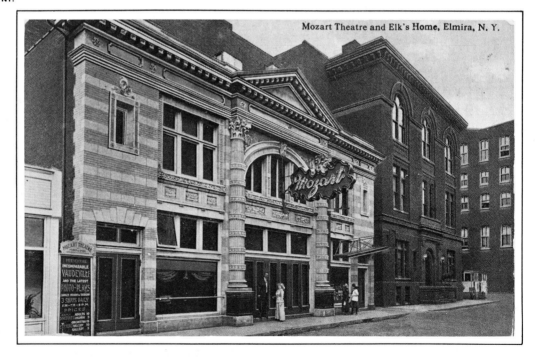

Mozart Theatre and Elk's Home, Elmira, N. Y.

When the Mozart Theater opened on East Market Street, east of Baldwin Street, November 23, 1908, 1,700 people were in the audience—300 were standees. Mr. George W. Middleton was the Resident Manager and Mr. Charles L. Roseberry was Orchestra Director. The theater was one of a chain of theaters opened as an actor-management cooperative. The actors group known as the White Rats of America, gave money to help build the theater created by Mr. Edward Mozart. Mr. Frank Tripp, of later newspaper fame, was the General Press Agent for the Mozart Circuit; also, Proprietor and Manager of the Royal Comic Opera Company which played in the Mozart for a few weeks during 1909. Seats for the Mozart shows cost 50 Cents for the first seven rows, 30 Cents for the first three rows in the balcony and 10 Cents for the gallery. No. 1 House Rule, *"Ladies are requested to remove their hats."*

The last legitimate show in the Strand—renamed from Mozart—was "A Streetcar Named Desire" during the 1951–52 season. One last performance was the Elmira Civic Chorus Spring Concert on May 16, 1959. The building was razed in 1967. To the right (East) of the Mozart, in this photograph, is the Elks Lodge, completed in 1911. Further to the right, partly visible on the corner is one of the many street lunch wagons in use at that time.

Publisher: Card No. A-44787, Horowitz Bros., Elmira, NY.
Manufacturer: Curteich Company, Chicago, IL.

The name of Steele has been associated with the Public Library in Chemung County since 1893. The name is based on the gift of Mrs. Esther Baker Steele in memory of her husband, Dr. Joel Droman Steele. The building was incorporated in 1893, cornerstone laid in 1895, and opened to the public in 1895. Dr. Steele amassed a modest fortune from the successful writing of textbooks, many with the help of his wife. With only an adopted son to consider, he had a goal of providing an adequate Public Library. However, he died before doing so. His wife put the plan into action by setting aside money from her annual income until the building fund was adequate for the construction of the building. A decision was made to erect a YMCA Building adjoining the East wall of the Library with one common roof. When the library opened in August 1899, throngs of people came to see the generous gift. Many brought their own gift of books for the library.

The first two floors of the original library were built around a center court, with columns around the court supporting the next floor. The court was topped by a skylight with colored glass. The books were kept in bookcases on the top two floors. The bookcases extended from the edge of the court to the walls of the building. The court was used as a reading room. The existing Steele (Chemung County) Library opened in 1979.

Publisher: Card No. 6538, Not Indicated.
Manufacturer: Not Indicated.

The Opera House was built on the Northeast corner of Lake and Carroll Streets. It opened in 1867 with a lecture by Mr. B. Gough. Mr. W. Charles Smith was the manager. Some of the important performances included: Ms. Laura Keene in "Our American Cousin" during 1867, Mr. Frank Mayo in "Davy Crockett" during 1873, and Mr. Edwin Booth and Mr. Lawrence Barrett in "Julius Caesar" during 1889. Mr. Samuel Clemens was Mark Twain in "The American Vandal Abroad" in 1868. The Opera House was remodeled in 1898 and the name changed to The Lyceum. It became the greatest theater in Elmira's history. Fire damaged the theater in 1904 and it re-

opened in 1905. From then until 1929 The Lyceum attracted large crowds with unusual performances. One of the most unusual performances was "Ben Hur" with real horses galloping on a noisy treadmill on the stage. The Lyceum closed in 1929. The site is now occupied by the Marine Midland Bank.

Publisher: Not Indicated.
Manufacturer: Not Indicated.

Y. M. C. A. Elmira, N. Y.

The planning meeting for the first YMCA in Elmira was held on June 29, 1858 at the Congregational Church then located in Ely Hall at 159 Baldwin Street. Young men representing six churches attended. The first proposal was to establish a reading room and lyceum for young men of Elmira, an association for social, moral, and intellectual achivement. The YMCA had a membership of 340 after 10 years. It supported the City Missionary and raised $2,500 to construct a chapel on Magee Street. In 1868, the headquarters were located in the Opera Block, 419 Carroll Street, at the corner of Lake Street. This photograph is looking East toward Lake Street shows the YMCA of 1895 on Market Street. On the building was an advertisement for the YMCA. Written on the outside brick wall, *"YMCA, NIGHT SCHOOL, Library, Educational Clubs, Gymnasium, Natatorium, Bowling Alleys, Baths, BIG MEETINGS FOR MEN SUNDAYS 3:30 PM, IT IS WORTH YOUR WHILE."*

Publisher: Not Indicated.
Manufacturer: Curteich Company, Chicago, IL.

The Hotel Langwell located on the Southwest corner of State and Market Streets was completed in 1896. It was built by Mr. Joseph Causer, a former superintendent of the Elmira Rolling Mills, who operated the old Elmira Hotel located on the West side of State Street near Water Street. Mr. Causer operated the Langwell until 1939 when he sold it. In the early advertisements, the Langwell offered 50 rooms with hot and cold water, 15 rooms with private bath, and rates of $2.00 to $3.00 per day. The Gotham Hotel located across Market Street was an annex of the Langwell from 1921-1929. The Langwell's English Grill and Rose Ballroom were very popular until the hotel closed in in 1959. In 1961, it was razed for the construction of Centertown.

HOTEL LANGWELL, ELMIRA, N. Y.

Publisher: Card No. R-79661, Rubin Bros., Elmira, NY.
Manufacturer: Curteich Company, Chicago, IL.

Christ's United Methodist Church, on Church Street, was organized as the Hedding Methodist Church in 1852. It was built on a site that was the residence of Mr. Erastus Babcock, attorney. The church shown was constructed in 1901 of Gothic design, with rock-faced stone and common bond brick. The interior stained glass windows were manufactured by the Pike Studio in Syracuse, New York. The present church congregation is the result of a merger between St. John's Methodist, First Methodist, and Hedding Methodist in 1968. The original Heddings Church building is now the Holy Trinity Lutheran Church.

Publisher: Card No. 106, Not Indicated.
Manufacturer: Not Indicated.

Elmira was served by volunteer fire companies until 1878. At that time, a paid company was formed. Much of the pageantry associated with the volunteer fire companies died at that time. The old names including, Torrent Fire Company 1, Neptune, Red Rover, Young American, Eureka, Ours 4, Goodell Hose Company, and Rescue Hook and Ladder Co. went into history. In 1890, the old building was razed and Fire Headquarters shown in the photograph was built on East Market Street opposite Exchange Place at a cost of $33,000. The site is now part of the facility used by the Star-Gazette Newspaper.

Publisher: Card No. 130, Baker Bros., Elmira, NY.
Manufacturer: Made in Germany.

VICTORY ARCH AND MAIN STREET, ELMIRA, N. Y.

The Victory Arch was constructed across Main Street at Wisner Park during a six-inch snowstorm. The work was ordered to be completed when information was received by the mayor of Elmira, Mr. Harry Hoffman, on March 28, 1919 that the veterans of World War I would arrive on April 1, 1919.

Publisher: Not Indicated
Manufacturer: Not Indicated

ST. JOSEPH'S HOSPITAL, ANNEX, ELMIRA, N. Y.

St. Joseph's Hospital was founded in 1908 in a remodeled school building on East Market Street. The building was a three-story Victorian structure with narrow windows and a gabled roof. This design was in sharp contrast to the newer building shown in this photograph, which was erected as an annex in 1914. It increased the hospital space to a 75-bed capacity.

Publisher: Rubin Bros., Elmira, NY.
Manufacturer: Tichnor Bros., Boston, MA.

Elmira, N.Y., West Church Street.

Hello Lola—I am having a nice time. don't this pretty. Mimie

The streets of Elmira give meaning and perspective to the history of the city and its people. At the lower right-hand side are two hitching posts and a carriage block at 460 W. Church Street, the home of the Fassetts. Across the street, on the Northwest corner of Church and Walnut Streets, was a large Second Empire home built for Mr. Eugene Diven in 1874. The son of General Alexander Diven, Mr. Diven was the Treasurer of American LaFrance Co. from 1878 to 1888. The Christian Science Church purchased the home in 1924 and used it as a reading room. The home was flooded in 1972 and burned in 1973. The church that now occupies the site was built in 1974.

Publisher: Card No. 4461, Miss Jeanette Adams.
Manufacturer: Made in Germany.

Maple Avenue, Elmira, N.Y.

Maple Avenue, named for the many maple trees lining the broad curbing on both sides, was one of Elmira's most fashionable addresses at the turn of the century. Many huge homes were located on this avenue including those built by Mr. John Brand, Sr., Mr. Daniel Sheehan, and Governor Lucius Robinson. Many of these homes exist today and some have been converted from single family homes to multiple apartment dwellings.

Publisher: Card No. 201886, Valentine Souvenir Company, New York, NY.
Manufacturer: Made in Germany.

ST. PETER AND PAUL CHURCH, ELMIRA, N. Y.

St. Peter and Paul's Church at 116 High Street was the first Irish Catholic Church located in Elmira. The initial construction cost in 1857 was $50,000. A window, located over the altar, comprised of special stained glass made in Germany, was installed later in the same year. An organ was installed in 1873 at a cost of $58,500. In 1926, a white Carrerra Italian marble altar was installed. It depicts the four Evangelists with statues of St. Peter and St. Paul located at the ends of the altar. A church of this magnitude and wealth constructed during the early part of Elmira's history reflects the large Irish population that was located in this area at that time. In 1916, the church was redecorated, the ceiling was painted in the same manner as many churches located in Europe.

Publisher: Not Indicated.
Manufacturer: Not Indicated.

American Sales Book Company began in 1896 based on a patent issued to Mr. Warren Beck for a duplicating sales book. In 1897, the Turnbull Shoe Factory, shown in this picture was purchased and converted to use by American Sales Book. Further expansion in 1906 led to the purchase of Elmira Steam Mill. In 1911, the company merged with Carter Crum Company. It became the Moore Business Forms in 1939 and operated until 1985.

AMERICAN SALES BOOK CO., ELMIRA N.Y.

Publisher: Not Indicated.
Manufacturer: Not Indicated.

Elmira Academy. Elmira, N. Y.

In 1859, the Elmira Free Academy, directed by Dr. Erastus Hart, offered free education for *"All those who could use it."* In 1865, a new building was constructed and Mr. Joel Dorman Steel was appointed Principal. He began an Honor Roll system, instituted English and History Departments, and made passage of the Regent Examinations compulsory. This building was razed in 1891 to provide space for a larger academy required by the increasing area population and enrollment.

Publisher: Not Indicated.
Manufacturer: Not Indicated.

ELMIRA FREE ACADEMY, ELMIRA, N. Y.

This school, originally the Elmira Free Academy, was completed and occupied in 1913. The excellent reputation of the school was the result of the faculty headed by the Principal, Mr. F. R. Parker. The students excelled in many fields and the graduates continue to hold top positions in many countries. In 1938, the school was refurbished and an addition was built on the North end of the building. The enlarged structure made it possible to offer industrial and commercial subjects to the students. The existing Elmira Free Academy located on Hoffman Street was built in the 1960's. The building shown in the photograph, is now known as the Ernie Davis Junior High School.

Publisher: Not Indicated.
Manufacturer: Not Indicated.

The Elmira Knitting Mills was established at Grand Central and Prescott Avenue in Elmira Heights in 1893 and continued until 1963. To encourage young girls to work in the company, the Conewawah Inn was built nearby. A matron was provided and the room and board were made available at a very reasonable cost. A working girl could expect to have 50 Cents remaining from her weekly pay for entertainment and recreation. A 1900 notice for the Inn listed a regular evening dinner at 15 Cents and 7 dinner tickets could be purchased for one Dollar.

Publisher: Not Indicated.
Manufacturer: Not Indicated.

The Elmira branch of the Kennedy Valve Mfg. Co. was established in 1907. The plant shown in this photograph was expanded several times with a brass foundry in 1920, and a 90,000 square foot warehouse in 1963. The plant was known for the manufacture of water hydrants, valves, and fittings. The family ownership ended in 1962 with the sale to the ITT Grinnell Corp. of Providence, Rhode Island.

Publisher: Not Indicated.
Manufacturer: Not Indicated.

Union Depot, Elmira, N. Y.

The Erie Railroad came to Elmira in 1849. The Chemung Railroad connected Elmira and Watkins Glen in 1849, and the Williamsport and Elmira Railroad began operations in 1854. In the beginning, all of these railroads used the Union Station as shown in this photograph taken in 1895. Within a short time the station became the Erie Railroad Station. It was closed to all passenger traffic in the 1970's.

Publisher: Not Indicated.
Manufacturer: Not Indicated.

LACKAWANNA STATION, ELMIRA, N. Y.

This Lackawanna Station was built in 1913 and abandoned in 1959. The first Lackawanna Railroad Passenger Train reached Elmira on April 3, 1882. On September 1, 1959, the Lackawanna and Erie tracks were consolidated. Passenger service was terminated in 1970.

Publisher: Card No. 106448, Rubin Bros., Elmira, NY.
Manufacturer: Trichnor Bros., Boston, MA.

In 1857, Dr. Edwin Eldridge, a medical doctor in Binghamton, NY, moved to Elmira where he spent the remainder of his life as an industrialist. He became involved in the management of the Erie and the Delaware, Lackawana & Western Railroad Companies bringing them into the Southern Tier. He was co-founder and president of the Elmira Iron and Steel Rolling Mills which operated from 1860–1888. In 1860, he purchased land for a park and after the Civil War he designed and supervised extensive filling, grading, and planting operations. He hired architect, Mr. Elisha Kingsbury to design and build an elaborate, six-story casino on the land. The park

Bird's Eye View of Eldridge Park, showing N. Y. State Reformatory in Distance, Elmira, N. Y.

also included fountains, lily ponds, a bandstand, footpaths, horse trails, a tree-shaded chapel grove, flower gardens, and a variety of amusement rides.

Dr. Eldridge died in December 1876 and the City of Elmira purchased the park for $37,500. A program of events for the week of June 9, 1902, lists a Wagner Family orchestra; G. J. Knightlinger, glass engraver; mini-theater marionettes; the Bijou circus; a trained animal act; and the Eldridge Park photographer. Dances and special events were to be held at the casino and animals were to be seen at the zoo. Among the other buildings were a penny arcade, shooting gallery, root beer stand, hot dog stand, and a large restaurant.

Publisher: Card No. C-22, Baker Bros., Elmira, NY.
Manufacturer: Not Indicated.

Home for the Aged, Elmira, N.Y.

A home to provide care for the Widows of the Civil War dead was established as The Home For The Aged. The Society For The Home For The Aged was incorporated in 1874. The construction was begun in 1877 and completed in 1879 because of the generosity of Dr. Edwin Eldridge. He and his wife donated land on Grand Central Avenue to the society. He later provided funds toward the structure. A colonial wing was added to the south of the main building in 1906 funded by Mr. John Brand in memory of his mother, who had always been interested in the future of the home. The conditions for admission to the home were an entrance fee of $150.00, sixty years of age, and a resident of Chemung County.

Publisher: Card No. C-34, Baker Bros., Elmira, NY.
Manufacturer: Not Indicated.

Woodlawn Cemetery was opened in July 1858. The major portion of the land was purchased from the farm of Mr. & Mrs. Charles and Mary Heller in the Northwestern part of Elmira. Mr. & Mrs. Israel and Frances Coates, Mr. & Mrs. Belorman and Ms. Polly Marsh, Mr. Legrange Bancroft, and Ms. Zera Compton were involved in this land acquisition which continued until 1920. A Mr. Daniels was hired to design the cemetery. The land was enclosed with a fence. Walks and drives were arranged in a serpentine design with space for planting trees and shrubbery.

During the dedication on October 9, 1858, the body of Colonel John Hendy, of

Civil War fame, was exhumed from the Old Baptist Cemetery and taken by Military procession for burial in Woodlawn.

Woodlawn is an outstanding example of the Park-Type cemeteries of the mid-1800s. On November 9, 1861, the cemetery was described in a newspaper article, *"In the whole plan, lines of beauty are only observed, every corner is rounded. Most of the avenues and paths wind and curve gracefully over the lawns, through the glens, down the declivities, giving full illustration that the course is truly the line of beauty. Surely amid such liveliness in sweetest security overlooking the busy hum but a little distant, none need fear to wrap the drapery of his couch around him and lie down in quiet unending rest."*

Publisher: Not Indicated.
Manufacturer: Not Indicated.

Mrs. Mariana Arnot Ogden gave Elmira its first General Hospital. The three-story building on Roe Avenue cost $75,000 and was given to the custody of a self-perpetuating Board of Managers for the benefit of the people in Elmira and vicinity *"Without regard to age, sex, color, creed, or nationality."* This photograph shows the hospital as of 1912. The hospital was opened on December 28, 1888 with 25 beds and a staff of three nurses, a matron, and four other employees.

Publisher: Card No. 216055, Not Indicated.
Manufacturer: Not Indicated.

Mr. J. Sloat Fassett born in 1853 distinguished himself as a lawyer, orator, industrialist, and politician. The son of Mr. Newton P. and Mrs. Martha Sloat Fassett, he lived in the family home at 460 W. Church Street until he built "Strathmont", as shown in the photograph, in 1896. Strathmont was located on 47 acres, with 53 rooms including 20 bedrooms. A pipe organ was located on the first floor near the main entrance. A private golf course was developed on the grounds and the men who played on this course were among the organizers of the Elmira Golf and Country Club in 1897.

Mrs. Fassett graduated from the Elmira Free Academy and the University of Rochester. The Fassetts were generous contributors to the building of the First Baptist Church and to the yearly charity balls in Elmira. The former Elmira College Dining Room and Fassett Commons were donations by Mr. Fassett. His library became part of a room donated by Mrs. Fassett in the college library. Strathmont was sold to Mr. and Mrs. J. Arnot Rathbone in 1928. They razed the old structure and built the current mansion, which is now owned by a developer.

"Strathmont", Fassett Homestead, Elmira, N. Y.

Publisher: Not Indicated.
Manufacturer: Not Indicated.

Chemung River from Bohemia Heights, Elmira, N.Y.

The area west of Fitch's Bridge to Mountain House was called Little Bohemia. Family type cottages were built in this area for boating and swimming purposes. This view is looking East from the Bohemia Heights.

Publisher: Card No. D3, Baker Bros., Elmira, NY.
Manufacturer: American.

This suspension bridge, built in 1922, is one span 440 feet long with nine large wire cables twisted and banded together. The cables swing from two massive iron uprights embedded in piers of rock. Total cost was $16,000 shared by the towns of Big Flats and Southport. The bridge was named for Mr. Daniel K. Fitch, one of the leading citizens of the area, who donated $2,500 toward its construction. It was destroyed by a flood in the 1930's.

Publisher: Metropolitan News & Publishing Company, Boston, MA.
Manufacturer: Made in Germany.

An important landmark was the Water Toboggan and Restaurant at Fitch's Bridge. Both were owned by Mr. and Mrs. John P. Frantz and located east of the bridge. The huge water toboggan attracted people from a wide area. One of the important rules was that *"Only persons in bathing suits were permitted to take the plunge into the river."* This photograph was taken in 1906.

Publisher: Not Indicated.
Manufacturer: Not Indicated.

Along the Erie R.R.

The steam locomotives of the Erie Railroad were an important part of the railroad transportation in and out of Elmira. The sight of these majestic Iron Horses has always been a pleasure to see. They were replaced by diesel locomotives in the 1950's.

Publisher: Card No. D7, Baker Bros., Elmira, NY.
Manufacturer: Not Indicated.

D., L. & W. R.R. BRIDGE, ELMIRA, N. Y.

The conversion from wooden railroad bridges to those made of iron and steel also brought changes in their design. Two important types of the designs using metal are the Panel Truss and the Howe Truss. The Panel Truss was designed by a military engineer Colonel Stephen Long in 1830 and its main feature is the use of an X-structure. Mr. William Howe introduced the Howe Truss in 1840 as a modification of the Panel Truss. Iron tie rods were used for the vertical members. The Howe Truss became the more popular design for railroad bridges. This bridge was the Newtown Creek Crossing of the Lackawanna Railroad located at the lower end of East Water Street, across from the Kennedy Valve Co.

Publisher: Rubin Bros., Elmira, NY.
Manufacturer: Not Indicated.

Bird's Eye View of Elmira, N. Y., from Mount Zoar.

Looking South along the Chemung River from Mount Zoar about 1915. Mount Zoar was also known as Fort Hill and Fort Henderson. Southern prisoners who escaped from the Elmira Prisoner-of-War Camp would make their way toward Mount Zoar to hide from the prison authorities.

Publisher: Not Indicated.
Manufacturer: Not Indicated.

Elmira College was founded on the concept:

"Due To An Earnest Desire of Christian Men and Women That Young Women Should Receive An Education Equal In Every Respect To That Offered Men".

Cowles Hall, named after Dr. Augustus Cowles, first president of the college, was designed by architect Mr. E. L. Barber and built by Mr. W. B. Ferrar in 1855. The entire college was housed in this octagon shaped structure offering economy in cost, functional design, and beautiful views from any of the eight exposures. Maximum air circulation was achieved with the open interior design and the ability to obtain a breeze from any external part of the

Elmira College.   Elmira, N. Y.

building with the three arms extending to the North, East and West. The extending one-story entrance on the East side was balanced by dormers projecting from the wings. During 1942–45, the chimneys and the porch on the south side were removed and the building lost much of its Gothic appearance.

Each young lady began her formal education with the curriculum for the First Session, First Year, including Elementary Greek Grammar, Algebra, Critical Reading of Thomson's Seasons, and Ecclesiastical History. The Second Session offered Cicero's Orations, Greek Testament, Botany, Critical Reading of Cowper, Philosophy, and History.

Publisher: Card No. 6257, Buffalo News Company, Buffalo, NY.
Manufacturer: Buffalo News Company, Leipzig, Germany.

Carnegie Science Hall, Female College, Elmira, N. Y.

The industrialist, Mr. Andrew Carnegie, donated this building to Elmira College. Construction was completed in 1911 and the design is an example of the work by architect, Mr. E. L. Tilton and represents the Neoclassical Revival design. The four-story building, with symmetrical window placement, has brickwork accenting the windows on the second and third stories. It was built at a cost of $60,000. In 1962, the Myrtle Picker Kolker Science Building and an archway were added to the south of the building. Carnegie Hall continues to be used for science studies.

Publisher: Not Indicated.
Manufacturer: Curteich, Chicago, IL.

The second building constructed after Cowles Hall was built in 1892 and named Gillett Hall. (Located in the center of this picture with the Carnegie Science Building to the right.) This structure was given to Elmira College by Mrs. Kate Mandeville Gillett in memory of her husband, Mr. Solomon Gillett. Mr. Gillett was an industrialist and banker, also a close friend and coworker of Mr. Simeon Benjamin, a founder of Elmira College.

9041. Elmira College Building, Elmira, N. Y.

The building was intended for the study of music. The college trustees, during a June 1891 meeting, were given a report on the new building, described as *"A two-story brick structure containing 22 teaching and practice rooms and lighted by electricity, heated by steam, and equipped with new pianos"*. The cost of the new building was set at $10,000. The structure is an example of Romanesque Architecture using a variety of construction materials including wood, brick, and stone. In 1958, the building was converted from music rooms to offices when the Watson Fine Arts Building was constructed.

Publisher: Card No. 9041, Not Indicated.
Manufacturer: Acmegraph, Chicago, IL.

ELMIRA COLLEGE, THE DINING HALL, ELMIRA, N. Y.

Mr. and Mrs. J. Sloat Fassett donated this building as a Dining Hall in 1917. Mr. Fassett was a lawyer, State Senator, a member of the House of Representatives, and a Trustee of Elmira College from 1879–1881 and 1894–1900. Mrs. Fassett was a College Trustee from 1915–1940. The structure, at a cost of $18,650, was built with the dining area on the second floor and the kitchen on the first floor. A bridge connects Cowles Hall to this building at the second floor. In 1965, the Campus Center was built and Fassett Commons was converted to classrooms and offices.

Publisher: Not Indicated.
Manufacturer: Not Indicated.

Elmira College Library, Elmira, N. Y.

3B-H189

Constructed in 1926, as a donation from Mrs. J. Sloat Fassett in memory of her husband, it was used to house the personal library of Mr. Fassett. The building was called "The Library". In 1940, it was renamed for Dr. H. Adelbert Hamilton, one of the admired members of the faculty and the community. In 1969, the Gannett-Tripp Learning Center was built and the Hamilton Library became Hamilton Hall for the Art Department. The local craftsmen were stone masons. The windows were imported from England, the brick came from Virginia, and the slate was obtained in Vermont. A fireplace decorated with the school flower, the Iris, memorialized alumna Lena Ford Brown, who wrote "Keep The Home Fires Burning". This building is an excellent example of collegiate style of Gothic Architecture with the sharp slate rooflines and projecting dormers.

Publisher: Card No. 3B-H189, Elmira News Company, Elmira, NY.
Manufacturer: Curteich, Chicago, IL.

Mr. Mark Twain—Mr. Samuel L. Clemens—are the magic names in the literary world and Elmira. Mark Twain's beginning with Elmira came when he married Miss. Olivia Louise Langdon in 1870. The international writer and humorist was considered an adopted Elmirian from the initial meeting with Mr. Charles J. Langdon in June 1867 during a cruise, and his first visit to the Langdon Home on August 24, 1868, until his burial in Woodlawn Cemetery on April 24, 1910.

Publisher: Not Indicated.
Manufacturer: Not Indicated.

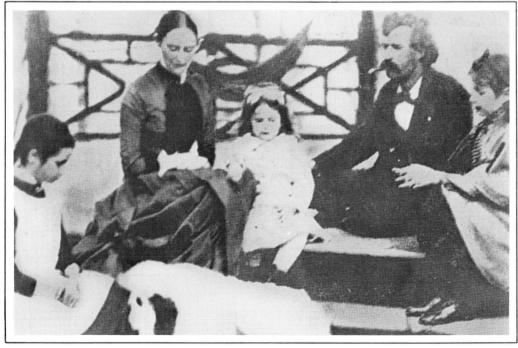

This photograph taken Circa 1882 includes Mr. Samuel L. Clemens, wife, and three daughters. Miss. Olivia Susan "Susy" Clemens was born in Elmira, March 19, 1872. Miss. Clara Langdon Clemens was born at Quarry Farms, June 8, 1874. Miss. Jane Lampton "Jean" Clemens was born in Elmira, July 26, 1880.

Publisher: Not Indicated.
Manufacture: Not Indicated.

A photograph of Mr. Mark Twain (Mr. Samuel L. Clemens) with Mr. John T. Lewis is the result of an interesting story. Mr. Lewis, an ex-slave, worked at Quarry Farm and had a few acres of his own in the valley behind Quarry Farm.

Mr. Lewis became a hero to the Clemens family. The young wife of Mr. Charles Langdon, her daughter Julia, and her nursemaid were in a buggy when their horse suddenly began speeding down East Hill toward Elmira. Mr. Lewis was homeward bound when he saw the runaway horse and buggy. He turned his team across the road, leaped from his seat, seized the bridle of the frightened horse and "Mighty of frame and

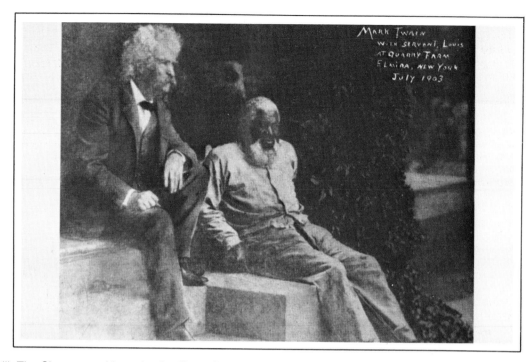

muscle" brought it to a standstill. The Clemens and Langdon families, who had seen the wild ride begin, arrived and found the people safe, and Mr. Lewis, the hero. He was given rewards of money, presents, and his long cherished dream of owning a silver timepiece *"Costing at least thirty Dollars."* When he was no longer able to work at Quarry Farm, he was given a pension to make the remainder of his life easier.

Publisher: Not Indicated.
Manufacturer: Not Indicated

Quarry Farm was the home of Mrs. Theodore Crane, the sister of Mrs. Clemens. The hilltop home, overlooking Elmira and the Chemung River, interested Mr. and Mrs. Jervis Langdon and they purchased it as a summer retreat for the family and relatives. There was an abandoned quarry partway up the hill and at the suggestion of the family minister, Dr. Thomas K. Beecher, the place became known as Quarry Farm. The home, located two miles from the center of Elmira on East Hill, was placed on the National Register of Historic Places on March 13, 1975. During the years of use the home was enlarged and a library was added in 1923. Mrs.

Mark Twain's Summer Home, Quarry Farm, East Hill, Elmira, N. Y.

7A H3675

Susan Crane built a study for Mark Twain near to the home. The home remained within the Langdon family until it was donated to Elmira College to be used as a writers' retreat and for American Studies.

Publisher: Card No. 7A-H3675, Rubin Bros., Elmira, NY.
Manufacturer: Curteich Company, Chicago, IL.

The study was built in 1874 for Mr. Mark Twain (Mr. Samuel L. Clemens) to have privacy in his work. He wrote to a friend, Mr. Twichell, *"It is . . . a cosy nest and just room in it for a sofa, table, and three or four chairs, and when the storm sweeps down the remote valley, and lightning flashes behind the hills beyond, and the rain beats on the roof over my head, imagine the luxury of it."* A letter to Dr. John Brown of Edinburgh adds a few details to this picture. *"The study is built on top of a tumbled rock heap that has morning-glories climbing about it and a stone stairway leading down through and dividing it. On hot days I spread the study door*

Study used by Mark Twain at Quarry Farm, East Hill, Elmira, N. Y. — 8

open, anchor my papers down with brickbats and write in the midst of the hurricanes, clothed in the same thin linen we make shirts of." In this study he wrote most of Huckleberry Finn, Tom Sawyer, and The Prince and The Pauper. In 1952, the study was moved from Quarry Farm to the campus of Elmira College.

Publisher: Not Indicated.
Manufacturer: Dexter Press, Pearl River, NY.

The Mark Twain-Gabrilowitsch Monument has an interesting background. Mr. Ossip Gabrilowitsch distinguished pianist and orchestra director, was the husband of Mrs. Clara Clemens Gabrilowitsch. He had asked to be buried at the feet of Mr. Mark Twain.

When Mrs. Clara Clemens Gabrilowitsch began to think of a monument for her father and husband she consulted Mr. Jervis Langdon II. He suggested contacting Mr. Enfred Anderson, an Elmira Artist. When the design was completed, the shaft of the monument was made of Western Granite, known as one of the finest stones. It was shipped to Qunicy, Massachusetts for finishing in the the hammered style. A highly polished panel was attached on the front of the shaft. Above the panel are bas-relief profile portraits, in bronze, of Messrs. Clemens and Gabrilowitsch. The shaft is exactly twelve feet or two fathoms high. Leadsmen on the Mississippi River Boats called out *"Mark Twain"* when the water was two fathoms deep. The moument weighs eight tons. On the base of the monument is the inscription, *"Death is the starlit strip between the companionship of yesterday and the reunion of tomorrow. To my loving memory of my father and my husband. CCG 1937."*

Publisher: Card No. 25526, Queen City Paper Company, Elmira, NY.
Manufacturer: Dexter Press, Pearl River, NY.

Grave of Mark Twain at Woodlawn Cemetery, Elmira, N. Y. — D-

35

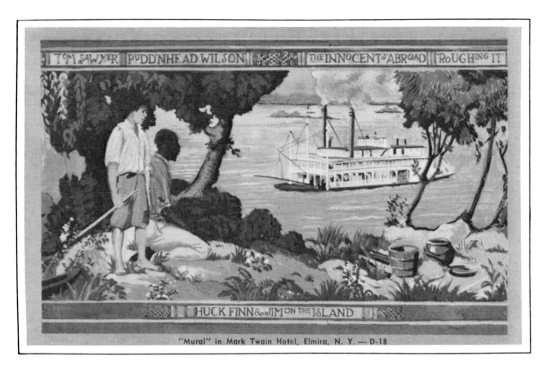

"Mural" in Mark Twain Hotel, Elmira, N. Y. — D-18

This mural, on the South wall of the lobby lounge in the Mark Twain Hotel in Elmira is the work of Mr. Arthur Crisp of New York City. It is 15 feet 3 inches by 7 feet 6 inches. The hotel was built in 1929 and was converted into apartments in the 1970's. The mural remains within the building.

Publisher: Card No. 25533, Queen City Paper Company, Elmira, NY.
Manufacturer: Dexter Press, Pearl River, NY.

Lake Street Bridge, Elmira, N. Y.   9052

This bridge was built in 1905 and replaced in 1961. During the time required to build the 1905 bridge, pedestrians crossed the river on a wooden structure located upstream. The base was concrete covered with paving brick and approximately 200,000 rivets were used in the Queen-Post type steel structure. The building on the right, across the river, is the warehouse and main office for the John Brand Co. and on the left is the F. M. Howell Co.

Publisher: Card No. 9052, Not Indicated.
Manufacturer: Not Indicated.

Mr. Fred M. Howell began this wooden cigar box business in 1883. He was president of the company for more than 50 years. In 1889 a label department was added and the printing of menus in 1895. After World War I, a folding box manufacturing line was begun and the company currently produces a wide range of packaging materials.

Publisher: Not Indicated.
Manufacturer: Not Indicated.

In 1873, Mr. John Brand, Sr. with Mr. Edmund Miller and Mr. Jacob Miller established a tobacco leaf business. The business grew on the basis of a cooperative tobacco marketing organization comprised of the growers. The success of the business is indicated by the fact that by 1875, Mr. Brand had built a large home at 355 Maple Avenue. The home remains today with numerous internal and external changes. The home was an outstanding example of the Queen Anne style, four stories, two decorative chimneys, two towers, a conical roof, and finials as shown in the photograph. The home was owned by Mr. John Brand, Jr. in 1879 when he inherited the business. In 1901, Mr. Brand donated part of his property to the City of Elmira and in return, Riverside Park or Buttonwood Park was renamed Brand Park.

Maple Avenue and Brand Homestead, Elmira, N.Y.

After the death of John Brand, Jr., the home was sold to Mr. Fred Knapp, contractor and builder, who lived in the home from 1932–1934, then it was converted into apartments. The home is currently owned by Mr. and Mrs. Harold Watts.

Publisher: Card No. A82, Baker Bros., Elmira, NY.
Manufacturer: Not Indicated.

RIVERSIDE PARK--FOUNTAIN AND BAND STAND, ELMIRA, N. Y.

The 22 ½ acres comprising Riverside Park, purchased by Elmira in 1901, are now known as Brand Park. The principal feature of the park is the Brand Park Swimming Pool. The original pool destroyed by the 1972 flood was replaced. The park has a picnic area, playground, and ball field.

Publisher: Not Indicated.
Manufacturer: Not Indicated.

Mayor Daniel Sheehan's Residence, Maple Avenue, Elmira, N. Y.

This home was built by Mr. Justus B. Harris in 1894 and is an example of the Queen Anne style as designed by architects Pierce and Bickford. Mr. Harris was one of the founders of Harris, McHenry and Baker Co. established in 1883. He also had large interests in two Southern lumber businesses. The imposing 19-room home, three stories, includes a large porch encircling two sides, and a porte cochere decorated with scrolled brackets. The porch is supported by Corinthian posts. Mr. and Mrs. Harris sold their home in 1903 to Mr. Daniel Sheehan. His large business, political, and civic activities caused the home to become known under his name. The wide range of his activities in Elmira made the home become a landmark. The Sheehans moved in 1936. The home had a series of owners and is now operated as a Christmas Home.

Publisher: Not Indicated.
Manufacturer: Not Indicated.

NEW SOUTHSIDE HIGH SCHOOL, ELMIRA, N. Y.

The development of industries on the Southside of the Chemung River resulted in the opening of new residential areas. The large influx of people led to the building of the Southside High School located at the intersection of South Main Street and Pennsylvania Avenue. It opened in 1924, with Mr. Frank Edson as Principal. This school offered the first complete industrial and commercial curricula in the area. A new Southside High School was built on South Main Street at the City line in 1978—80. The original building is now used for the Chemung County Human Resources Center.

Publisher: Not Indicated.
Manufacturer: Not Indicated.

RESIDENCE OF SAMUEL D. AULLS, 225 WILLIAM ST., ELMIRA, N.Y., FORMERLY OWNED BY GOV. DAVID B. HILL,
DEEDED FROM HILL TO COL. GABRIEL L. SMITH, HIS LAW PARTNER AND PURCHASED (1907) BY AULLS.

David Bennett Hill was born in Havana, New York (now Montour Falls) in 1843. At 20 years, he came to Elmira to study law in the office of Tierston, Hart & McQuire. He was admitted to the bar in 1844 and became a partner of Judge Gabriel L. Smith. In 1870, he became the largest investor in the Elmira Gazette. In 1882, he was elected Mayor of Elmira. He was elected Governor of New York in 1885. Samuel D. Aulls was a lawyer with an office at 214 East Water Street. The home shown in the photograph has been razed.

Publisher: Not Indicated.
Manufacturer: Not Indicated.

St. Mary's Church and Convent, Elmira, N.Y.

St. Mary's Church on the Southside of Elmira, was begun in 1872 as the parish for an expanding Irish congregation in Elmira. The construction was hampered by many difficulties. Severe storms caused the unfinished walls to fall on two occasions. The second collapse resulted in the death of one man and injury to 14 men. In 1877, a fire caused a ten per cent loss of the structure. In the interim, the parish has become the largest in Elmira. The parochial school was founded approximately in 1880 and in 1898, a new brick school building was constructed for the children attending the Convent school. The Convent building, shown on the right, is not owned by the church today. The building is used as an administrative headquarters for the Glove House, a home for youths.

Publisher: Not Indicated.
Manufacturer: Made in Germany.

Elmira, N.Y., Old Hendy Cabin—First House in Elmira, 1790.

As one of the first settlers of Elmira, Mr. John Hendy, or Colonel John Hendy as he became known, built this cabin in West Elmira across from Roricks Glen in 1796. Colonel Hendy was prominent at all public occasions. For example, in 1831, at the age of 74, he dug the first shovel of dirt for the Chemung Canal.

Publisher: Not Indicated.
Manufacturer: Not Indicated.

The fame of Elmira as a fire engine capital began in 1873, with the founding of the LaFrance Manufacturing Co. Mr. Truckson LaFrance, a young man with an inventive mind, came to work at the Elmira Union Iron Works and by 1871 and 1872, he had obtained several patents on improvements for rotary steam engines. Mr. John Vischer, the head of the Iron Works, was encouraged to make a steam fire engine and within a short time Messrs. Vischer and LaFrance were operating a small business producing fire engines.

Among the many novel designs for American LaFrance, as the company became known, was a Spring Rising Aerial Ladder

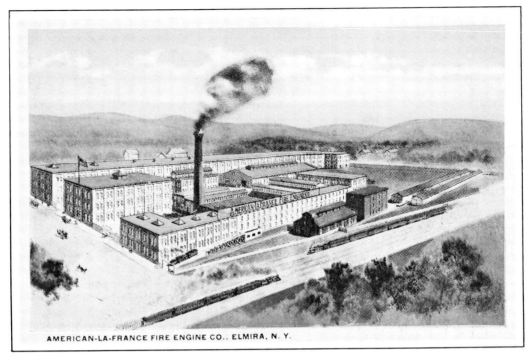

AMERICAN-LA-FRANCE FIRE ENGINE CO., ELMIRA, N. Y.

Truck invented by Asa LaFrance, Banty Wright, and A. Ward LaFrance. The latter later founded the Elmira Heights Fire Apparatus Company under his own name. By the 1890's, the LaFrance fire equipment had a coast-to-coast market and later became world-wide. The World Wars led to wide use of the fire equipment. In 1955, Sterling Precision Corporation acquired American LaFrance and in 1966 sold it to Automatic Sprinkler Corporation. During the last decade, the business was acquired by Figgie International and it was moved to Virginia. The Elmira plant closed in 1985.

Publisher: Rubin Bros., Elmira, NY.
Manufacturer: Not Indicated.

The popularity and usefulness of American La France equipment is well known. One example of the worldwide usage of the equipment in the earlier days of the company is shown in this photograph. The acquisition of a new "Pumping Engine" in 1913 at Juneau, Alaska obviously created a great deal of pride and interest among the members of the Juneau Fire Department.

Publisher: Not Indicated.
Manufacturer: Not Indicated.

Gleason Sanitarium, Elmira, N. Y.

Dr. Silas O. Gleason and his wife, Dr. Rachel Brooks Gleason established the Gleason Health Resort on Watercure Hill in 1852. The reputation of the healing establishment was based on the use of baths and sprays as a water cure. The Gleasons left the resort in 1898 to be with their daughter in Buffalo, NY. Drs. Theron and Zipporah Wales served at the resort from 1873 to 1897 and were succeeded by Dr. John C. Fisher. Later the resort was converted into a nursing home. The building was razed in 1959.

Publisher: Not Indicated.
Manufacturer: Not Indicated.

The golden age of Roricks Glen was from 1901 to 1917. For the area, it was unique in two approaches to having fun. No liquor was sold and it became an unusual artistic center. There were free unreserved seats for the trolley car patrons. The people with more money to spend had season tickets with seats in the reserved section. Picnic grounds were available and many families dined before the performances. The 1200 seat theater was open on three sides and canvas could be raised or lowered as the weather required. The backstage included scenery with rain and snow making equipment. The theater was advertised as the most elaborate open-air playhouse in the country.

RORICK'S GLEN THEATRE, ELMIRA, N. Y.

Roricks Glen began with vaudeville and minstrels and later featured the Manhattan Opera Company. The beginning of the automobile and competition from the motion pictures led to a decline in patronage. The gorge was topped with an earthwork remains of a fortification that has been dated as pre-Iroquoian. The old wooden bridge connecting the West Water Street trolley car loop with Roricks Glen was replaced by a steel bridge in 1907. This bridge was washed away in the 1946 flood and the bridge that was built in its place was carried away in the 1972 flood. Roricks Glen closed in 1918 and the theater remained closed. It burned in 1932. The dance pavilion was used in the 1960's as a Boy Scout facility and it was razed for safety reasons in 1976.

Publisher: Not Indicated.
Manufacturer: Not Indicated.

In 1869, New York State pased a law authorizing the establishment of an institution for the holding of the male offenders between 16 and 30 years of age who had never previously been convicted of a crime. The location for this reformatory was Elmira. The reformatory opened in 1876 on 16 acres near the Northwestern boundary of the city. Later, a 280-acre farm located in Big Flats was operated in conjunction with the reformatory. This institution was the first reformatory in the world and the first penal institution to accept prisoners with indefinite sentences. Mr. Zebulon R. Brockway was the creator of the reformatory. He worked in Penology all of his life. Mr.

View in Enclosure, — showing group visitors, New York State Reformatory, Elmira, N. Y.

Brockway considered that punishment alone, without rehabilitation, was useless. As superintendent for the first 24 years, he added shops and factories within the walls. Most of the people who worked in these operations manufactured items for resale.

In 1888, a building was completed for trade classes; by 1894 the curriculum included 600 inmates in 34 trade classes. Also, reading, writing, arithmetic, and geography were included in the courses. A band and military-type organization were established for dress parades. Escorted tours of the reformatory were very popular for many years and people made a stop at the reformatory as part of a trip in the area. The towers and chimneys were removed during the 1940—1950 period and the reformatory is now a Maximum Security Prison.

Publisher: Not Indicated.
Manufacturer: Not Indicated.

"Zim" is the name affectionately given to Mr. Eugene Zimmerman. He is considered to have been the best known citizen of Horseheads. Before his death in 1935, he had a reputation for his lampoon-type portrayals of the important people in his time. This work occurred in his 1911, "A Foolish History of Horseheads" and his later "A Foolish History of Elmira." He also created a bandstand, located in Teal Park, covered with wooden creatures playing various types of musical instruments.

One of his epitaphs, written in The Chemung Valley Reported, referred to him as, "Horseheads' outstanding and most beloved citizen, and international cartoonist, who spread happiness thruout the world as few men have . . ."

Publisher: G. A. Treat.
Manufacturer: Not Indicated.

Zim's Residence, Horseheads, N. Y.
Pub. by G. A. Treat

Today, except for the tower, this building in Montour Falls is the home of the New York State Academy of Fire Sciences. As a result of a twist of fate, the building did not become the site of a college, and perhaps a stumbling block to the founding of Cornell University in Ithaca, 30 miles away.

During the early 1950s, plans were being made for the financing of a *"College For The People."* Mr. Charles Cook, a New York State Senator, from what was then the Village of Havana, became interested in founding a school, as was Mr. Ezra Cornell. After listening to the proponents of this college, Mr. Cook is reported to have expressed

Cook Academy, Montour Falls, N. Y.

the wish "To make a Little Oxford of Havana." He pledged the necessary land and a large sum of his personal money to help raise the public funding that was required. The cornerstone laying ceremony was on September 2, 1858. Mr. Cook created anger in some people who wanted the Land-Grant College in their own areas. In 1863, Mr. Cook suffered a debilitating stroke and developed a perverse attitude. He did not have a family or close associates to carry on with the college effort and the grant went to Mr. Erza Cornell. The building became known as Cook Academy and was used as a Boarding High School before public education was readily available to all communities.

Publisher: Not Indicated.
Manufacturer: Made In Germany.

Chequagah Falls, Montour Falls, N. Y.

When water courses over this stone face at the West end of main Street in the Village of Montour Falls . . . or when winter sculpts the scene . . . Chequagah Falls is beautiful. This photograph was taken before the Federal Government began a flood control project to halt the frequent floods that had affected the village. When the stream of water was diverted, the village landscaped an attractive park below the falls. A tradition states that the famous Seneca Orator, Mr. Red Jacket, practiced his speaking while standing before the roaring waterfall to perfect his ability to be heard when addressing hundreds of people. Another tradition states that Louis Philippe, later King of France, sketched the beauty of She-Qua-Ga (Chequagah) in 1820. This piece of art supposedly hung later in the Louvre in Paris. There is some evidence that the King's Brother was the artist. The Louvre officials disclaim any knowledge of this work of art.

Publisher: Commericalchrome.
Manufacturer: Not Indicated.

Odessa, in the Town of Catharine, is centrally located in the Eastern side of Schuyler County. It is one of the county's four self-governed villages. This photograph was apparently taken while July Fourth or another National Holiday was being observed as noted by the array of flags. Mr. P. L. Gabriel, whose name is on the second store from the left, began business here in 1904. The local telephone company was located on the second floor of the same building. Three ladies known as the *"Kellogg Triplets"* named Margaret, Mellee, and Anna were in charge of the switchboard.

Publisher: Not Indicated.
Manufacturer: Not Indicated.

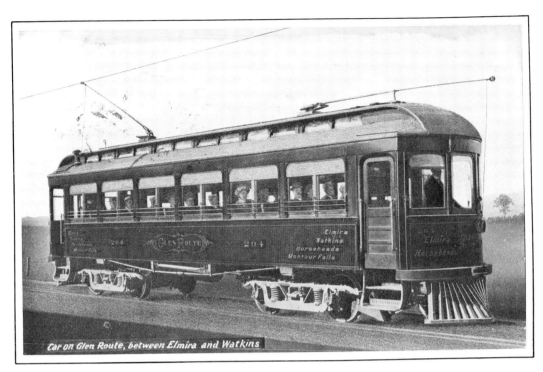

Car on Glen Route, between Elmira and Watkins

The planning for the Elmira and Seneca railway began in 1895. A considerable number of obstacles had to be overcome before the first trolley began to run on June 6, 1900 because of political considerations. The oak and chestnut ties and steel rails were laid on the Tow Path of the defunct Chemung Feeder Canal. According to the early publicity, a smooth ride was assured because no grade exceeded four percent. The powerhouse and car barns were located in Millport in Chemung County. The railway was abandoned in November 1922.

Publisher: Card No. A33, Baker Bros., Elmira, NY.
Manufacturer: Not indicated.

The Glen Springs Hotel was a Health Spa. The saline and mineral waters were believed to have curative powers for many ailments including chronic heart problems. Although the Indians, native to the area, had used the salt seeps found on the Seneca Lake Hills for medical purposes, the spas were created after the speculators had financed drilling in the search for natural gas. The resulting salt and mineral formations began the spas with small buildings, which added more rooms with their success, until the buildings grew to the size shown in this photograph. During the years when silent movies were made in Ithaca, the fashionable trip for the

The Glen Springs Hotel, Seneca Lake, Watkins, N. Y.   1813

movie stars was to spend time at Glen Springs taking a cure for whatever bodily ailments bothered them. The use of the spa declined after 1925 and following World War II, the building was used to house Veterans (and their families) attending Cornell University and other nearby colleges. Later it was used as a Preparatory School for young Catholic Priests and continues to be used as classrooms for noncredit courses.

Publisher: Card No. 1813, Not Indicated.
Manufacturer: Not Indicated.

Seneca Lake and State Highway, near Watkins Glen, N. Y.

106958

Route 14 on the West side of Seneca Lake was changed from a dirt road to a concrete surface, in a project that began in September 1914 and completed in October 1918. The road ended approximately five miles from the Northern border of Watkins Glen. Another similar road, along the East side of Seneca Lake, was built in part by road gangs comprised of prison labor.

Publisher: Card No. 106958, R. C. Pomeroy, Watkins Glen, NY.
Manufacturer: C. T. American Art, Chicago, IL.

Seneca Lake from Glen Kissingen Spring, The Glen Springs.   Watkins, N. Y.

Hand-Colored.

During the years that Glen Springs was popular as a health resort, several of the springs were individually housed and labeled according to an analysis of the water contents. Different minerals were classified for curing specific ailments. The scenery in the area was beautiful and there was a variety of exercise and recreational activities available including golf. The name Watkins used on this postcard was a correct designation for the Village of Watkins until 1926 when the name Watkins Glen was approved by the U.S. Post Office.

Publisher: The Albertype Company, Brooklyn, NY.
Manufacturer: Not Indicated.

The Magee Residence was considered a showplace in Watkins Glen. The home was begun in 1869 for General George Magee (Retired). He and his son John brought life to Schuyler County when they built a railroad to transport coal from their Pennsylvania mines to Seneca Lake coal barges and, as a result, opened the markets. Watkins Glen acquired its present Presbyterian Church because of the generosity of the Magees. Other benefits from the Magees included the giving of the estate by deed to the Village. The estate was sold in 1946 for $10,100. It was subsequently used as a home for girls, later as a youth hostel, and then as an apartment house. The estate reverted to Village ownership for nonpayment of taxes. Over the years there was huge deterioration in the property and the property was razed in 1960.

Publisher: Eagle Post Card View Company, New York, NY.
Manufacturer: Not Indicated.

ENTRANCE TO WATKINS GLEN, WATKINS GLEN, N.Y.

79398

The main entrance to Watkins Glen State Park is approximately ten blocks south of Seneca Lake on Franklin Street, which is the main street in Watkins Glen. The arch shown in the photograph was razed in 1936 to make the entrance to the park look more modern. A short distance beyond the entrance is the new Timespell Laser Light and Sound Show. This display is seen at night, in good weather, projected against the stony cliff located a short distance into the gorge.

Publisher: Card No. 79398, Hope Souvenir Shop, Watkins Glen, NY.
Manufacturer: C. T. American Art, Chicago, IL.

Entrance and Old Mill
(50 years ago),
Watkins Glen, N. Y.

The 1909 postmark on the address side of this postcard provides an approximate date for the Grist Mill that was located near the main entrance of Watkins Glen State Park. The mills built previously were located at higher points in the glen to utilize the natural waterfalls for power. This mill was operated with water diverted from the upper creek through a raceway. The drilled access hole, for the water, was located near the entrance bridge and fancifully called "The Bear Cave." The mill burned during 1910. The bridge shown in the right center of the photograph is on Route 14 or Franklin Street in Watkins Glen.

Publisher: Gates & Hurley, Watkins Glen, NY.
Manufacturer: Not Indicated.

One of the many spectacular waterfalls in the Watkins Glen State Park is called "Rainbow." At specific times during a sunny day, the waterfall lives up to its name with a beautiful rainbow to thrill the visitor. At this viewpoint, as shown in the photograph, the path through the glen takes the visitor underneath the waterfall.

Publisher: Card No. 10689, J. D. Hope, Watkins Glen, NY.
Manufacturer: Litho-Chrome, Germany.

Rainbow Falls, Watkins Glen, Watkins, N.Y.

Watkins Glen.   Winter Scene.   Watkins, N. Y.

The beauty of the Watkins Glen Gorge in the Winter is unfortunately not available for viewing. The ice formations that transform it into a blue-green wonderland also creates extremely hazardous conditions for the visitor. As a result, the glen is closed during the winter period.

Publisher: Card No. 6544, Rochester News Company, Rochester, NY.
Manufacturer: Leipzig, Germany.

Copyright 1905 by the Rotograph Co.
5085 a. Upper Entrance and N. Y. C. R. R. Bridge, Watkins Glen, N. Y.

Handcolored.

A photograph taken from the Upper Entrance of Watkins Glen State Park in 1906. The railroad tracks on this trestle were originally built for the Fall Brook Railroad and were extended North from Watkins Glen in 1878. The railroad became known as part of the New York Central Railroad and is now part of Conrail. The 175-foot high trestle was washed away during the flood in 1935.

Publisher: Card No. 5085a, Rotograph Company, New York, NY.
Manufacturer: Germany.

Transportation on Seneca Lake was important to travelers, commerce, and recreation. The boats were numerous and many did not survive for any great length of time. Also, many of the boats were renamed and the records became confusing. The SENECA shown in this photograph was built in 1849. The boat used a sidewheel and propeller. Among the many tasks assigned to the SENECA were, the transportation of Northern troops, moving during the Civil War, from the South end of the lake to Geneva. She was used in a limited operation as a ferry boat between Dresden on the West side of the lake and Ovid Landing on the East side of the lake. The operation was not a financial success and was cancelled. In later years the boat was renamed the OTETIANA.

Publisher: Not Indicated.
Manufacturer: Not Indicated.

During the time when Steamboating on Seneca Lake was considered an important event, the Sagoyewatha Inn at North Hector (Valois) Point was a favorite resort. The Goodwin Ferry provided passage from this point across Seneca Lake during an era when the trip, on foot or on a horse, was an overnight journey. The veranda, encircling the building, was quite satisfactory for the vacationers who wished to sit in a rocking chair and enjoy the view. It was also was used as a dance floor. The Inn was built by a group of businessmen, a majority from Watkins Glen, and passed through several owners. In 1918, the Inn, ice house, and two barns were destroyed by fire.

Publisher: The Valentine Souvenir Company, New York, NY.
Manufacturer: Not Indicated.

A photograph taken today—from the same place that this photograph was taken—in the Village of Burdett high above Seneca lake on an East Hill, would include the Fire Station. The Fire Station facing Main Street would occupy a site on the right side of the Mill Pond shown in this photograph. This pond was created when the creek was dammed for a mill. Several small creeks come into the main waterways from Logan and Texas Hollow passing through Burdett to Seneca Lake. The pond was destroyed during the 1935 Flood.

Publisher: Not Indicated.
Manufacturer: Not Indicated.

This photograph of the International Salt Company located on Salt Point Road, North of Watkins Glen at the edge of Seneca Lake, was taken in 1912. This period was one of the rare times when Seneca Lake was frozen to considerable depth. The extensive salt bed that is beneath Schuyler County and extends into parts of Pennsylvania, Ohio, West Virginia, Michigan, and Southern Ontario was located in 1882. Drillers looking for natural gas, petroleum, salt, and other minerals discovered the extensive salt bed at a depth of approximately 1800 feet. Some of the early salt mining operations closed many years ago. This plant began the salt operations in 1899 and has been modified during recent years in conjunction with the changes in mining methods. Another salt company, Cargill, is located within Watkins Glen at the South end of the lake.

Publisher: Not Indicated.
Manufacturer: Not indicated.

Eagle Cliff Fall, Havana Glen, N.Y.

Havana Glen has been known through many decades in Schuyler County. Havana Glen has developed and rivaled what is now Watkins Glen State Park. Although this glen is less accessible to the public, it has beautiful waterfalls, pools, and little dells that are scenic wonders. The Iroquois Indians used Havana Glen as a place for meetings, ceremonies, and important rituals for their culture. According to one archeologist, part of a ceremonial turtle remains in the glen. The glen is now owned and operated by the Town of Montour and it is used for family reunions, rustic camping, and has a children's playground.

Publisher: Card No B13319, Buffalo News Company, Rochester, NY.
Manufacturer: Leipzig, Germany.

On July 11, 1929, a Westbound Erie train was partly derailed including a tank car filled with gasoline. Before the signals could be set for other trains, an Eastbound Passenger train crashed into the wreckage and the spilled gasoline was ignited by the hot coals from the locomotive of the passenger train. The fire spread quickly killing the engineer, fireman, two mail clerks, and a hobo in one of the cars. Although the wreck occurred outside of the city, the Corning Fire Department responded to the wreck; however, there was very little they could do as no water was available in the area. These two photographs illustrate typical train wreck scenes that occurred too frequently.

Publisher: Mrs. J.H. Freeman, Savona, NY.
Manufacturer: Not Indicated.

Publisher: Not Indicated.
Manufacturer: Not Indicated.

Corning, N. Y., The Crystal City

Country Club

106952-N

In September 1919, a group of interested gentlemen bought the Coger Farm outside of Gibson in order to build a country club with a golf course. Work was begun immediately. In the Fall of 1921 a record was established for the first game played on three holes at the rudimentary course. The clubhouse burned in July 1952 and the members decided not to rebuild the clubhouse. They prepared plans to build a new and larger country club.

Publisher: Card No. 160952N, Lamb's Pharmacy, Corning, NY.
Manufacturer: Curteich Company, Chicago, IL.

Picnics, band concerts, baseball games, canoe rides, early aviation flights, and a large number of other recreational activities have been available for many years in Corning's Denison Park. The park began to take substantial form in 1906 when the Corning Businessman's Association purchased land—known as the Johnson Property—located in the Eastern part of Corning to build a park for the people of Corning. A New York City Architect, Mr. A. Caparn, was hired and plans were prepared for the park. Mill Street bordering the property had its name changed to Park Avenue and construction of the park began in April 1907. Mr. Charles L. Denison gave

8512. Denison Park, Corning, N. Y.

$10,000 in the memory of his Father to prevent work stoppage because of a shortage of funds. The deed to the park was presented to Mayor McNamara by President George Showers of the Corning Businessman's Association on September 6, 1909.

A zoo was added to the park in 1909. Several improvements were added in 1910 including a ball field, running track, children's playground, concrete bridge, pavilions, drinking fountains, and a 90-foot wading pool with a central bronze fountain provided by Mr. James A. Drake. The park closed in 1917.

Publisher: Card No. 8512, Not Indicated.
Manufacturer: Not Indicated.

Glass cutters monument

This monument located in St. Mary's Cemetery was erected by the American Flint Glass Workers Union as a memorial to Corning Glass Workers who were killed in a railroad disaster in Ravenna, Ohio. The monument was unveiled on September 16, 1893, to commemorate the employees who died. They were traveling because the plant had closed for the annual summer vacation. The men were in a chartered railroad coach being used to bring them home from Ohio. At 2:30 AM, a fast freight train struck the wooden coach, it burst into flames, and 17 of the 44 men—ranging from 16 to 26 years of age—were killed. The men were given a common service at Harvard Hall and then more than 100 carriages led the funeral procession for the burial.

Publisher: Not Indicated.
Manufacturer: Not Indicated.

The Soldiers' Monument was dedicated to Civil War Veterans on Memorial Day in 1911. Approximately 10,000 people gathered at the corner of 1st Street and Park Avenue to see the 40-foot high, 56-½-ton statue unveiled. Corporal Tanner of Washington DC, former Commissioner of Pensions, delivered an address and a parade of patriotic and civil societies and school children completed the event.

Publisher: Curteich Photochrome, Chicago, IL.
Manufacturer: Curteich, Chicago, IL.

Mr. H.P. Sinclaire was active in the management of the Corning Glass Works and the Hawkes Rich Cut Glass Works. When the latter was reorganized into the T.G. Hawkes and Company, he became its Secretary. Mr. Sinclaire left the company in 1904 and established his own business of producing cut glass. There were at least 12 companies in the cut glass business at that time. The plant was built with much attention to the aesthetic qualities and landscaping. His cut and engraved glass became widely known for the introduction of new ideas and designs. The plant closed in 1927 after his death and was sold to the Cobakco Company in 1930 to operate as a modern baking company.

FACTORY OF H.P. SINCLAIRE & CO. CORNING N.Y.

Publisher: Not Indicated.
Manufacturer: Not Indicated.

School No. 2,
Corning, N. Y.

Pub. by The J. M. Greig Co., Corning, N. Y.

School No.2 was constructed at a cost of $15,000 in 1883. It was located on First Street to be used for primary grades. In recent years the building was converted for use by the Corning City School District Administration Offices until the offices were moved to the former Painted Post High School/Grammar School site.

Publisher: J.M. Greig Co., Corning, NY.
Manufacturer: United Art Publishing, New York, NY.

East First Street as viewed from Pine Street. This beautiful residential street was the first East-to-West Street South of Erie Avenue and is now called Denison Parkway.

Publisher: Card No. E25631A, Rotograph Company, New York, NY.
Manufacturer: Made In Germany.

Looking west on Third Street from Cedar Street provided a view of a very fashionable location. Many wealthy residents of Corning lived here in large Queen Anne style homes.

Publisher: Not Indicated.
Manufacturer: Not Indicated.

The Corning City Hospital began with a serious debate pertaining to the need for a hospital in February 1893. During a public meeting in March, tentative plans were made for a 15-bed, $23,000 hospital. During April 1896, local women developed a Hospital Fair Association. The first Hospital Fair produced $2,058.39 and by 1899 they had raised $3,480.43.

On January 26, 1900, the Stearn Family offered their homestead at 159 East First Street on a rent free basis for three years. The Hospital Association treated 105 patients in the first year. In 1902, the Stearn Family sold the property to Mr. Franklin D. Kingsbury and he gave it to the Hospital

Association. In 1903, a new building was required. Mr. Amory Houghton bought the O'Conner house at 91 Erie Avenue and offered the property to be used as a hospital. The new three-story hospital shown in the photograph was built and it opened on October 10, 1905.

Publisher: Card No. 13632, Souvenir Company, New York, NY.
Manufacturer: Made in Germany.

This imposing structure constructed of local brick and terra cotta was designed by Mr. Henry G. Tuthill and built in 1893-1894. It replaces an earlier church built in 1861. This church was the First Methodist Episcopal Church and is now the United Methodist Church located at 1st and Cedar Streets. The Corning Daily Journal, on August 15, 1894, states: *"Since the completion of the new elegant First Methodist Episcopal Church of this city, Mr. H. G. Tuthill & Son have been meeting with great success as church architects. The cost was more than $40,000 including the organ."*

Publisher: Not Indicated.
Manufacturer: Not Indicated.

The Episcopalians had established a Mission Church in Corning by 1840. In 1854, they built a stone church on the corner of Erie Avenue and Walnut Street. By 1890, they were looking for a location on which to build another church. After an unsuccessful effort to obtain land in Court House Square, a decision was made to build at the corner of First Street and Pine Street.

The Christ Episcopal Church was built using stone from a local quarry beginning with the laying of the cornerstone in November 1893. The church was dedicated in 1895 after a cost of $60,000. Almost $100,000 was spent after the inclusion of the finish-

A 25627   Christ Church, (Episcopal), Corning, N. Y.   a. g. Smith.

ings including a Tiffany Window showing the ascession of Christ. Mr. John Hoare later contributed another Tiffany Window. The first ceremony in the church was the marriage of Actor, Mr. Otis Skinner to Miss Durben on April 2, 1895. They were the parents of Ms. Cornelia Otis Skinner. The church had a fire in February 1910. After the fire, Tiffany & Company, New York City, made $15,000 in repairs to the building including six new stained glass windows.

Publisher: Card No. A25627, The Rotograph Company, New York, NY.
Manufacturer: Made In Germany.

On March 30, 1898, the City Club was opened and became an exclusive social center. During the Spring of 1926, the building was gutted by fire and the members decided not to rebuild the interior of the building. They moved the club to the Baron Steuben Hotel. A group of citizens raised $75,000 to rebuild the structure into a memorial library, which remained in operation for more than 40 years.

Publisher: Card No. 13629, Souvenir Post Card Company, New York, NY.
Manufacturer: Made In Germany.

World War Memorial Library, Corning, N. Y.

On Memorial Day, 1930, this building was dedicated as a library and World War I Memorial, interested citizens raised $75,000 by public subscription to buy and remodel the fire-damaged City Club. The rennovated structure became an attractive library and perpetual living memorial. In 1931, Mr. Frederick Carder designed a panel cast in yellow Bristol Glass with the names of the war dead. The building was used until a new library was built in 1975.

Publisher: Not Indicated.
Manufacturer: Not Indicated.

Court House, CORNING, N. Y.

In 1853, Steuben County was divided into two Jury Districts and a court was convened in Corning during 1854. A brick courthouse was built in the square. In August 1903, the Drake Company was given a contract to build a new courthouse in the square. It was built on the Southwest corner of Pine Street and First Street for a cost of $25,000.

Publisher: Card No. 13027, Souvenir Post Card Company, New York, NY.
Manufacturer: Made In Germany.

St. Mary's Convent. Corning, N. Y.

Castles are buildings that create legends and Corning had a castle perched on a hill overlooking the river. An act of the New York State Legislature on April 15, 1857 appropriated $14,000 for the Arsenal. The contractor, Mr. James M. Hawley completed the building in 1858 for $12,900. The massive building, with its native stone walls, was built with a castle design. The front view is part of the design of the emblem for the U.S. Corps of Engineers.

The building was used for the storage of State Ordinance and as a headquarters of Companies C and D, 60th Regiment of the New York State Militia. During the Civil War the Arsenal was used as a staging point for troops enroute to Elmira for mustering. In 1873, New York State decided to sell the building and it was purchased by Mr. Jeremiah Liddy and Captain John O'Shea for $12,000. They planned to have Corning businessmen invest in facilities for making shoes in the building. The plan failed and St. Mary's Parish purchased the building as a convent for the Sisters of Mercy and the headquarters for the St. Joseph Orphan Asylum. The remodeled building was ready in 1875. In 1906 a new convent was built and the Arsenal remained empty until 1965 when St. Mary's Parish sold the land around the building and the ruins of the Arsenal were razed for the building of the Castle Garden Apartments.

Publisher: Card No. B12665, Buffalo News Company, Buffalo, NY.
Manufacturer: Lithochrome, Leipzig, Germany.

For well over a century, St. Mary's large stone edifice has been the main landmark of Corning's Irish Hill. The first wooden structure known as St. Mary's Catholic Church was dedicated on July 24, 1849 at First and State Streets in the center of the Irish community. After the Civil War, the Catholic Parish decided to build a new church facing State Street between 2nd and 3rd Streets. Ground was broken in 1866 and the church was sufficiently completed in March 1869, in time for a St. Patrick's Day Fair. The church was blessed on Sunday, June 12, 1870 and dedicated on October 8, 1871. The dedication brought a special train of 12 cars from Elmira, crowded

ST. MARY'S CATHOLIC CHURCH AND NEW CONVENT, CORNING, N. Y.

with people, on the Erie Railroad. Another special train from Bath and other intermediate stations was also used to handle the huge crowd of people. The convent was added to the church in 1906.

Publisher: Card No. A72345, Not Indicated.
Manufacturer: Not Indicated.

New York Central and Hudson River Railroad Bridge. Corning, N. Y.

This bridge was used by the New York Central Railroad to connect the Northside and the Southside of Corning. The Brick, Terra Cotta Company is visible to the right of the bridge across the river. At the right side of the bridge is a small boy holding himself up against the end of the structure. We can assume that he could not resist the temptation to climb on the framework of the bridge.

Publisher: Card No. B12663, Buffalo News Company, Buffalo, NY.
Manufacturer: Litho-Chrome, Leipzig, Germany.

"Erie Ry." Bridge over Chemung River, Corning, N. Y.

This Erie Railroad bridge was built in 1876 to replace a wooden bridge. It was razed when the Erie Railroad tracks were moved.

Publisher: Card No. A107055, S.H. Knox & Company, Buffalo, NY.
Manufacturer: Made in U.S.A.

Messrs. A. S. Cook and J. S. Suffern sold groceries, crockery, and other typical grocery store items at 118 Pine Street as listed in the 1903 City Directory. In 1907, Mr. A.S. Cook was no longer in the business and Mr. J.S. Suffern was listed as the sole proprietor. We can surmise that the fresh pineapples scattered on the front center of the floor must have been newly received and the gentleman standing at the right side of the photograph—holding a pineapple—must have been working with them.

Publisher: Not Indicated.
Manufacturer: Not Indicated.

Messrs. J.J. Shepard, C.E. Rose, and L.L. Conover sold gas, plumbing supplies, bicycles, talking machines, sporting goods, and picture framing at 107 Bridge Street. Also, note the items placed outside the store on the sidewalk including coils of hose, kerosene heaters, mats, and two Morning Glory Horns.

Publisher: Not Indicated.
Manufacturer: Not Indicated.

Hermans and Lawrence Building and Elks' Club, Corning, N. Y.

The Corning Elks Club began in 1892. By 1907, there were 35 members but, no local lodge. On May 10, 1907, Corning Lodge 1071, Benevolent and Protective Order of Elks was established. Dr. Henry Agree was the Exalted Ruler with 225 members. They were established in a building at Denison Parkway and Pine Street which had long been a Corning Landmark. Messers. Hermans and Lawrence began the construction of a three-story building at what was then Erie Avenue and Pine Street. This site was the location of the old Exchange Hotel. The Elks Lodge held their meetings in this building. The building was damaged by fire in 1913. The tenents at that time included, the Evening Leader, Corning Laundry Company, Ferris Glass Company, and Canfield Brake Company.

Publisher: Not Indicated.
Manufacturer: Not Indicated.

Y. M. C. A. Building, Corning, N. Y.

The YMCA Building located at the Northeast corner of Market and Cedar Streets was dedicated on May 8, 1892. Two bowling alleys were added to the building in 1907. A storm damaged the upper floor and the building was remodeled into a two-story building. After the YMCA vacated the building it was used by the Corning Savings and Loan Association and later became part of the Columbia Bakery. At the time this photograph was taken, the United States Express Company was located in the front corner of the building. Also, note the decorative Lunch Wagon parked at the curb. The photograph shown below is another view of Market Street.

Publisher: Not Indicated.
Manufacturer: Not Indicated.

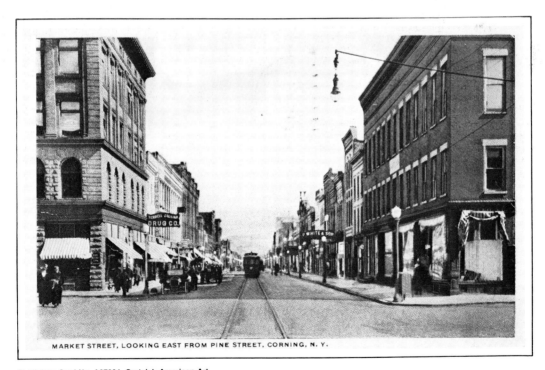

MARKET STREET, LOOKING EAST FROM PINE STREET, CORNING, N. Y.

Publisher: Card No. A67034, Curteich American Art.
Manufacturer: Curteich, Chicago, IL.

Greigs
Department Store,
Corning, N. Y.

The Greig Department Store had two locations. The last location was in a building located on the North side of Market Street between Pine and Walnut Streets. It became the Rockwell Department Store in November 1922.

Publisher: Card No. 10438, Buffalo News Company, Buffalo, NY.
Manufacturer: Litho-Chrome, Leipzig, Germany.

Greig Dry Goods Co. Bld'g. Corning, N.Y.

Publisher: Not Indicated
Manufacturer: Not Indicated

Market Street, Looking West, Corning N.Y.

Market Street has always been Corning's Commercial Center. In addition to retail stores it has been a home to residences, hotels, restaurants, banks, churches, and manufacturers of cut glass, candy, and cigars. The disastrous fires of the 1850's destroyed numerous buildings and caused Corning's Commercial Center to change from wooden structures to brick and stone. During the years of Corning's growth, the street has changed with different businesses and residents. In 1878 , a sidewalk was added and in 1883, the street was paved. By 1889, Corning was the only village in Steuben County with paved business streets.

In 1896, transportation in Downtown Corning was mechanized with the use of trolley cars. During 1972, a professional restoration plan for Market Street was accepted by the City Government. From that time, Market Street has been developing with the best available aesthetic designs maintaining a historical framework, and working for commercial potential. This photograph must have been taken at a time when the lady dressed in fashionable clothes was able to push her baby carriage on the sidewalk without disturbing other pedestrians and without the problem of traffic on the street. The photograph shown below was in one of its happy moods.

Publisher: Baker Bros., Elmira, NY.
Manufacturer: Made In Germany.

A Gala Day, Market Street, Corning, N.Y.

Publisher: Buffalo New, Company, Buffalo, NY.
Manufacturer: Litho-Chrome, Leipzig, Germany.

Dirt street scene looking South from the Corner of Pine Street and Erie Avenue. On the right side of the photograph is the Corning Opera House and visible in the distance on the left side is part of the First Presbyterian Church.

Publisher: Card No. C13974, Buffalo News Company, Buffalo, NY.
Manufacturer: Leipzig, Germany.

The First National Bank was established by Messrs. Franklin N. Drake, George B. Bradley, and Charles C.B. Walker in 1882 in the Greig Department Store building located on the Northeast corner of Market and Pine Streets.

Publisher: Curteich Photochrome.
Manufacturer: Curteich, Chicago, IL.

Pine St. North from First St. Corning N. Y.

City Club.   Opera House.   Town Clock.   Presbyterian Church.

Looking North on Pine Street, the City Club is on the left side of the photograph and the Opera House is located beyond the City Club. The First Presbyterian Church is on the right and the Clock Tower is visible in the distance.

Publisher: Tom Jones, Cincinnati, Ohio.
Manufacturer: Not Indicated.

In 1891, The Corning Opera Company built the Conservatory of Music and Opera House on the West side of Pine Street between First Street and Erie Avenue. The H.O. Dorman Company completed the construction for $33,306. The gala first-night opening on October 8, 1891, had excellent box office receipts of $1,240.30.

Many plays and musicals were performed and the performers included Ms. Julia Marlow, Ms. Maude Adams, and Ms. Cornelia Otis Skinner. Later the performances also included minstrel shows, local benefits, town meetings, and various celebrations. During December 1904 a boxing match was staged and women were permitted to attend. The Corning Free

Corning Opera House and Conservatory of Music, Corning, N.Y.

Academy graduation ceremonies were performed here from 1892 to 1923. Beginning in the 1930's, and continuing until the 1950's, motion pictures were shown. The building was razed and the site is now occupied by the F.W. Woolworth Company.

Publisher: Baker Bros., Elmira, NY.
Manufacturer: Made In Germany.

Innovation Soda Fountain
at
O'Hara's Opera House Pharmacy
Corning, N. Y.

This pharmacy was located on the ground floor of the Corning Opera House and Conservatory of Music. It later became the Richardson Tea Room, a very popular eating place. The Innovation Soda Fountain (O'Hara's) was a highlight of the pharmacy as described in 1903 advertisments:

"Choice imported and domestic cigars, the best of everything in the drug line, Bottomely's Ice Cream—the finest made—at the Opera House Pharmacy.
If you want the finest confectionary get it at O'Hara's.
O'Hara's Ice Cream Parlor is the swellest in the city.
Your prescription is accurately compounded at the Opera House."

By 1917, O'Hara's was no longer listed in the City Directory.

Publisher: Not Indicated.
Manufacturer: Not Indicated.

CASALE'S HOTEL AT CORNING, N.Y.

Corning's railroads brought great prosperity to the City. The Erie-Lackawanna Railroad running through the center of town was especially important. Erie Avenue became a prime location to build restaurants and hotels to take advantage of the railroad business. During 1907, Mr. Thomas D. Casale obtained the Minot House on Erie Avenue. The building was remodeled and expanded, and reopened as the Casale Hotel on June 18, 1908. The hotel was located on Pine Street and Erie Avenue adjacent to the Erie Railroad Depot.

Publisher: Not Indicated.
Manufacturer: Not Indicated.

ERIE DEPOT, CORNING, NEW YORK.

The first Erie Railroad train passed through Corning in 1849. The Erie Depot located at the Northwest corner of Pine Street and Erie Avenue opened during the summer of 1860. A single set of tracks was expanded to two sets of tracks in 1863. The original depot was enlarged a number of times because of the increasing passenger travel between New York City and Buffalo, New York. The depot was razed after World War II, when the Erie Railroad moved its tracks from passing through the city to a point near the Delaware, Lackawanna, and Western tracks crossing the Chemung River. A number of hotels were built near the depot to accommodate the growth of passenger travel. Note the prominent sign for the ORLANDO HOTEL at the right side of the photograph.

Publisher: Not Indicated.
Manufacturer: Not Indicated.

Eggington's Glass Cutting Shop, Corning, N. Y.

The T.G. Hawkes & Company which manufactured cut glass opened in 1890. Mr. H.P. Sinclaire, Mr. Oliver F. Egginton, and Mr. T.G. Hawkes (Foreman) became partners. Mr. Sinclaire as the secretary of the company was permitted to purchase a 12-½% share of the company. Mr. Egginton received one share of stock by subscription. Mr. Egginton left T.G.Hawkes in 1897 and began his own company, the O.F. Egginton Rich Cut Glass Works in a new plant located at State and 5th Streets. In October 1898, a two-story addition was added to the building to meet the demand for the excellent quality cut and engraved glass that Mr. Egginton produced.

Publisher: Not Indicated.
Manufacturer: Not Indicated.

New Post Office Building, Corning, N. Y.

The U.S. Post Office building was dedicated on January 10, 1910 at the corner of Erie Avenue and Walnut Street. By 1914, the mail for Corning had grown to the volume where Corning was classified to have a First Class Level Post Office.

Publisher: Card No. M2700, The Buffalo News Company, Buffalo, NY.
Manufacturer: Made In U.S.A.

City Hall, Corning, N. Y.

Corning became an incorporated city in 1890. Pride and need soon led to the building of a City Hall. On March 16, 1891, petitions signed by more than 600 taxpayers were presented as a request for a building to be erected as a general municipal building to include offices, a jail, quarters for firemen, a fire station, and a public hall. In 1892, the Common Council approved plans for a City Hall. A contract was awarded to Thomas Bradley & Company of Corning for $28,579.50. The building was completed in November 1893. The opening consisted of a fair and sale conducted by Pritchard Hose Company and the Protectives Company during December 11-16, 1893. The building is now the home of the Rockwell Museum.

Publisher: Card No. 219051, The Valentine-Souvenir Company, New York, NY.
Manufacturer: Not indicated.

THE FRANK B. HOWER SCOTTISH RITE CATHEDRAL, CORNING, N. Y.

Masonic activity in the Chemung Valley reaches back at least to the time of the Sullivan-Clinton Campaign. Corning Masons were presented with a special gift which enabled them to build this Frank B. Hower Scottish Rite Cathedral near to the Elks Club on Walnut Street in 1919. The cornerstone was laid on December 6, 1919. On November 18, 1920 the Annual Meeting of the Corning Consistory Scottish Rite Masons was held in the new cathedral and approximately 850 Masons were advanced to the 32nd Degree.

Publisher: Not Indicated.
Manufacturer: Not Indicated.

Court House Park, Corning, N. Y.

The Corning Company, the original organizers of Corning, set aside Block 66 to be used as a Public Square. For years it hosted churches, a school, and a court house. In 1905, the Common Council ordered Mr. R. H. Canfield, City Engineer, to prepare plans for the use of Court House Square as a park. Mr. Canfield submitted his plans to the Council in January 1906. The plans specified three plazas, a bandstand, gravel walks, shade and ornamental trees, and park benches. In 1906, the grading and sodding were begun, the walks were installed, and trees and shrubs were planted. A concrete fountain, 25 feet in diameter was added in 1909.

Publisher: Card No. A17030, S. H. Knox & Company.
Manufacturer: Not Indicated.

The German Evangelical Church on West First Street was built in 1908. The history of the church is based on the Protestant Germans who were looking for their own church and in 1895 established the German Evangelical Church in the former Christ Episcopal Church at the southwest corner of Erie and Walnut Streets. In 1906, a decision was made to build their own church. When the old church was taken down, its walls were used in the construction of the new church shown in the photograph. The cornerstone was laid June 28, 1908.

Publisher: J.M. Greig Company, Corning, NY.
Manufacturer: United Art Publishing, Germany.

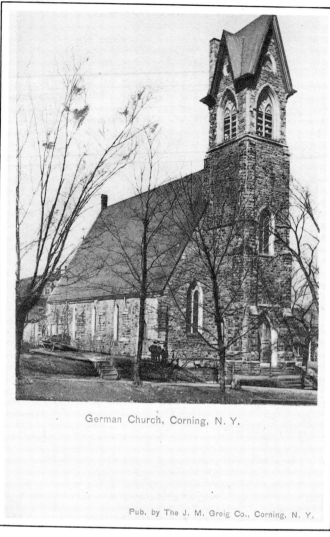

German Church, Corning, N. Y.

Pub. by The J. M. Greig Co., Corning, N. Y.

School No. 3, Corning, N. Y.

School No. 3 was located on the Northwest corner of Chemung and 5th Streets. After it ceased being used as a Public School, it was occupied by the Corning Community College for classroom space, until a new college campus was built on the Spencer Hill Site.

Publisher: Card No.W36928, Curteich Photochrome.
Manufacturer: Curteich, Chicago, IL.

The Corning Free Academy and Union School was built in 1873 at the cost of $70,000. It was located at the Northwest corner of Walnut and 3rd Streets on a portion of nine lots purchased by the school district. The first session of school was held on Monday, September 1, 1873. The bell in the tower, made by the Meneeley Foundry, West Troy, New York, was 50 inches in diameter and weighed 2500 pounds. The building was made of red brick, with a 70 × 100 foot foundation. A subcellar basement included a coal room and the furnace. The main basement contained six rooms occupied by the janitor and his family. Every room had gas burners. More than 100 gas burners were included in the entire building.

CORNING FREE ACADEMY, CORNING, N. Y.

When School No. 3 was built in 1909, Corning Free Academy became a High School. In 1910, Manual Training was added for Grades 1 through 8, including various types of shopwork, sewing, weaving, patching, and darning. The building was condemned and razed in 1934.

Publisher: S.H. Knox.
Manufacturer: Made In Germany.

ST. MARY'S PAROCHIAL SCHOOL, CORNING, N. Y.   33

St. Mary's Parochial School was built as St. Mary's Academy in 1881 and located across from St. Mary's Church on West First Street. The building included a gymnasium, basketball court, and a swimming pool. The building was modernized in recent years and is now being used as a school for primary grades.

Publisher: Card No. 120200, Teichnor Quality Views, Middletown, NY.
Manufacturer: Not Indicated.

A 25640 Third St., looking East, Corning, N. Y.

East Third Street looking East from Walnut Street. The former residence of Mr. Arthur A. Houghton, Jr. (at the right side of the photograph) was built circa 1900. To the East of the Houghton Residence is the home of H.P. Sinclaire. Mr. Houghton donated his home to the College Center of The Finger Lakes in 1962. The Corning Free Academy is now located on a site directly across the street.

Publisher: Card No. A25640, Rotograph Company, New York, NY.
Manufacturer: Made In Germany.

In 1915, Mr. Quincey W. Wellington, and Mr. Frances C. Williams helped Mr. Alanson B. Houghton to acquire 18 acres of land on the hill south of Corning. The land became known as the *"Highland Pines Sanitarium"* owned by Mr. Allen E. Klopp of Buffalo. Mr. Houghton planned to build the *"Finest residence to be found in the Southern Tier."* approximately, $40,000 to $50,000 was spent to acquire the property known as the *"Knoll"*. In August 1916, newspapers reported that Architect Howard Greenley had designed a *"Magnificent Country Estate"* for Mr. Houghton. *"The house is to be built of Corning Brick, in modern English Style, including twenty-two rooms,* eight rooms for servants, eleven baths, and a hot water heating system. Mr. R.S. Russell of Buffalo is to complete the house in 1917 at an estimated cost of $50,000."

AMBASSADOR HOUGHTON'S RESIDENCE AND GARDENS, CORNING, N. Y.   106951

Publisher: Card No. 106951, Not Indicated.
Manufacturer: Not Indicated.

Liveryman William J. McPherson drove this bus to carry passengers between the Pine Street Square business district and the Delaware, Lackawanna, and Western Railroad Station. The New York Central Passenger Station was located on the Pine Street Square, two blocks from Erie Avenue and the Erie Railroad tracks. The station was adjacent to the Dickinson House. Mr. McPherson has a very interesting business name shown in the photograph, *"U or Ure Baggage, Corning, N.Y."*

Publisher: Not Indicated.
Manufacturer: Not Indicated.

Prior to the building of the Memorial Bridge in 1920, Centenary Square was known at various times as The Pine Street Square and The Dickinson House Square. The square was a special place. Evangelists, politicians, and salesmen eagerly came to speak to the crowds that gathered here. People came here for the news, mail, gossip, and recreation. On the left side of the photograph is the Dickinson House and the New York Central Railroad Station. On the right side is the Drake Block purchased by the First National Bank. The J.M. Greig Department Store was on this site for many years.

Publisher: Baker Bros., Elmira, NY.
Manufacturer: Made In Germany.

CORNING, N. Y.

N. Y. C. AND
H. R. R. DEPOT

TOWN CLOCK

CORNING GLASS WORKS

"I erected the Clock Tower in the Village of Corning and placed in it a clock for the purpose of presenting them to the village in grateful rememberance of the village being named after my Father and of the interest he had and felt in its properity"
Erastus Corning

Plans for the gift of a memorial clock were made in 1882. It was designed by a Rochester, New York architect and work was begun in May 1883 by a local builder, Mr. John Cogan who constructed the tower of local stone. During December 1883, a bell weighing 1400 pounds was installed and the clock, produced by a French clockmaker, was installed in January 1884. With the exception of one temporary move, the memorial clock and tower have stood at Corning's center during all of these years.

Publisher: Card No. 13625, Souvenir Postcard Company, New York, NY.
Manufacturer: Made In Germany.

The Dickinson House was begun in 1850 by Mr. Hiram Bostwick and Mr. Andrew B. Dickinson. (Mr. Dickinson later became Ambassador to Nicaragua under President Lincoln). A newspaper description of the hotel on September 3, 1851, *"This spacious hotel will be opened this week for the reception of travellers. It is an ornament to the village and there is occasion for congratulations."* The square in front of the hotel became known as Dickinson House Square and was the social and political center of the community. A social trend was established that the Dickinson House was the important place to visit. The hotel was demolished in 1927 when the Baron Steuben Hotel was built.

MARKET STREET, SHOWING DICKINSON HOUSE, CORNING, N. Y.   32

Publisher: Card No. 120199, CHNOR Quality Views.
Manufacturer: Not Indicated.

Baron Steuben Hotel

7A-H2615

The Dickinson House on the Pine Street Square had a long reign with an outstanding reputation in the Southern Tier. Its central location and fame for hospitality had made it an attraction to local residents and visitors. During March 1927, a newly formed hotel corporation including Mr. Amory Houghton, Mr. Arron J. Williams, and Mr. E.S. Underhill, announced plans for a new hotel to replace the 1850 Dickinson House on the same site.

The Corning Evening Leader, September 1928, said of the Baron Steuben Hotel, *"Although . . . accomodations and service are equal to the best in the large modern hotels in the metropolitan cities, the prices for meals and rates for rooms will be within reach for all."* A single room without bath was available for $2.50 per night with more luxurious accomodations costing $5.00. The majority of the 100 rooms had baths or showers and all had toilet facilities. Bathrooms were finished in white tile and marble. Dinner was served in the main dining room and a less expensive meal was served in the coffee shop. Hooked rugs covered the terrazzo floors and the lighting fixtures were described as *"Old tallow candles glorified by the art of the electrician, the artistic glass manufacturer, and the wrought iron worker."*

Publisher: Card No. 7A-H2615, C.T. Colortone.
Manufacturer: Curteich, Chicago, IL.

The Corning Glass Works was contracted to produce a 200-inch glass disc to be used as the reflecting mirror for the Mt. Polomar Observatory in California. The disc required very special characteristics including hardness to withstand scratches, the ability to accept a high polish, resist contraction and expansion caused by temperature changes, and strength to resist sagging because of its 20-ton weight. This piece is the largest single glass object that has been cast and it was made of Pyrex. The first casting was imperfect as a mirror blank because of mold problems. However, it was useful to test the glass annealing process. A second and perfect casting was

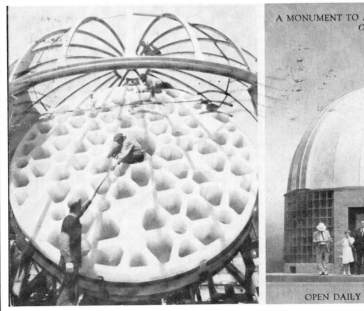

A MONUMENT TO ASTRONOMY AND TO GLASS
Corning, N. Y.—"The Crystal City"

OPEN DAILY 9:00 A. M. TO 10:00 P. M.

made on December 2, 1934. A replica of an observatory was constructed in the square located in front of the Baron Steuben Hotel to display the first disc. In January 1951, the disc was moved to the Corning Glass Center.

Publisher: Not Indicated.
Manufacturer: Not Indicated.

Ground was broken for the first building of the Corning Glass Works on June 8, 1868. The company was established by Mr. Amory Houghton, formerly proprietor of the Brooklyn Flint Glass Works in Brooklyn, N.Y. The railroads were useful for the Corning Glass Works with the intersection of the Erie and New York Central tracks on the site. Much of the success for the company was also based on the products that were developed for use by the railroads. The market was large because of the extensive railroad expansion that occurred throughout the U.S. during the 1870's. In 1877, Mr. Charles Houghton designed and patented a railroad signal lens with in-

Corning Glass Works, Corning, N. Y.

side corrigation and a smooth exterior surface that resisted dirt, snow, and ice that would normally buildup. The company also developed standardized colors for railroad signal lenses.

In the 1880's, a major new product was developed by producing the bulb blanks for Mr. Thomas Edison's new electric lamp. The Corning Glass Works became the major producer of the bulb blanks. The plant shown in the photograph was expanded in 1888 with two additional furnaces and 104-foot high chimneys. In 1889 another chimney was added and in 1890 an additional two chimneys were added.

Publisher: Card No. 219058, Valentine Souvenir Company, New York, NY.
Manufacturer: U.S.A.

The first railroad station in Steuben County was the New York Central Railroad Station shown in the left foreground. The Corning Glass Works is located to the right. This station was built in 1881 for the Fall Brook Company. It was a replacement for the original station built in 1840 and used by the Blossburg-Corning and Tioga Railroad. The New York Central acquired the railroad in May 1899 and the combined system became known as the New York Central Pennsylvania Division. The tracks shown in the photograph are no longer in existence and the station and the land around it became a municipal parking lot. Many times artistic license is used to en-

CORNING GLASS WORKS, CORNING, N. Y.

hance the photograph. For example, the U.S. Flag shown in the foreground is being blown toward the building while the smoke in the background is being carried in another direction.

Publisher: Card No. A72342, Curteich American Art, Chicago, IL.
Manufacturer: Curteich, Chicago, IL.

The Corning Glass Center was a Corning Centennial Project. It was dedicated by Governor Thomas E. Dewey on May 19, 1951. The complex includes the Hall of Science and Industry, the Steuben Factory, and the Corning Museum of Glass. The Corning Glass Center was designed by Mr. Mies van der Rohe and is faced with sheets of photosensitive glass, plate glass, and glass blocks. The connecting bridge between the Hall of Science and Industry and the Steuben Blowing Room was made of bent Pyrex brand tubing. A 36-foot diameter cylinder in the Science Hall was made of curved sheets of plate glass. The Corning Glass Center

also has a large auditorium, which is used for antique and modern car exhibits, important dance events, auctions, summer theater, and many other events.

Publisher: Card No. 1C-P1982, Arthur H. Richards, Watkins Glen, NY.
Manufacturer: Curteich, Chicago, IL.

This interesting scene of the Corning Glass Works was incorrectly labeled as The Corning Cut Glass Company. The latter was incorporated in 1901 by Mr. James Sebring. He advertised the product as *"The cut glass that makes Corning famous."* The Corning Glass Works began legal action in 1902 to restrain Mr. Sebring's company from using its name and slogan on the grounds that both were used to mislead and deceive the public. The suit continued for nine years and was decided against the Corning Glass Works in 1911.

Publisher: Baker Bros., Elmira, NY.
Manufacturer: Made In Germany.

The T. H. Symington Co's. Bridge St. Plant, Corning, N. Y.

In 1904, the T. H. Symington Company of Baltimore opened facilities in Corning to manufacture brake shoes and car boxes. By the end of 1904, they were operating two local factories and had purchased a foundry on East Market Street. The total employment was more than 200 men. In December 1904, the company opened a branch foundry in the Corning Stove Works building. On April 18, 1906, the main plant on East Market Street was badly damaged by fire.

Publisher: L.T. Gooderidge, Corning, NY.
Manufacturer: Made In Germany.

Sedimentary bedrock left by an ancient inland sea became a valuable material for the Corning Brick Works established in 1878 by Mr. Charles A. Rubright. He was a veteran of the Civil War and a survivor of imprisonment in the Andersonville Prison. By 1889, the demand caused by the Victorian love of ornamentation required the Brick Works to add decorative terra cotta to its products.

In 1896, Mr. Morris E. Gregory bought the company and changed the name to the Corning Brick and Terra Cotta and Supply Company. The brick and terra cotta produced by this company can be seen on hundreds of buildings in the Corning area. Local streets

A 25632 Brick Works, Corning, N. Y. 3/2/07.

and sidewalks were made of Corning Bricks and many areas outside of Corning also used the products of this company. A fire in July 1921 caused a layoff of 75 workers in the brick making part of the company.

Publisher: Card No. A25632, The Rotograph Company, New York, NY.
Manufacturer: Sol-Art Prints, Germany.

In 1907, the Wing and Bostwick Company, was located at 79-81-83-85 Bridge Street, advertisements provided a good indication of what was important in retailing:

"'Money Back' is the motto at the Northside. If the goods are not right bring them back and get your money back . . .

We buy and sell for cash and give you more for your cash.

Clothing, Hats, Caps, Shoes, Rubber Goods, Furnishing Goods Department First Floor.

The largest and best equipped grocery department in the city. Finest goods and lowest cash prices. Prompt delivery. Both Phones . . .

Interior View, Wing and Bostwick Store, Corning, N.Y.

A complete line of new furniture at rock bottom prices. Third Floor. Take elevator.

Corning's pride is 'The Northside' the most up-to-date and absolutely the largest department store in Steuben County.

Ladies, every street car stops at the big Northeast Department Store. A car every 10 minutes."

The store went out of business in the 1930's.

Publisher: Card No. 1325, Shepherd, Rose & Conover, Corning NY.
Manufacturer: Made In Germany.

North Side Baptist Church, Corning, N. Y.

The North Baptist Church was completed and dedicated on July 12, 1906 on Jennings Street. The church remains at the same location with several additions made to it during recent years.

Publisher: Card No. A17044, S.H. Knox & Company, Buffalo, NY.
Manufacturer: Not Indicated.

The newly organized First Congregational Church held services in its chapel on the Northside of Corning during November 1890. In 1892, the congregation built a parsonage on Decatur Street. The cornerstone for a new $21,000 church on Ontario and Bridge Streets was laid on October 2, 1896 and the building was dedicated on May 13, 1897. A newly installed pipe organ cost $10,000 of which $1,200 was donated by Mr. Andrew Carnegie in 1906.

Publisher: Not Indicated.
Manufacturer: Not Indicated.

In 1920, the Northside Grammar School had 870 students, 38 percent of the total school population. There were three separate school districts within the city limits. Southside, District 9; Northside, District 13; and the Parochial System. The school registration in 1920 was the largest ever recorded with 300 in the Corning Free Academy; 753 in District 9 Grammar Schools No. 1, 2, and 3; 285 in the Northside High School; and 870 in the Northside Grammar School. The Parochial Schools had 29 percent of the enrollment. At that time many of the boys and girls had finished their formal education after completing the eighth grade.

Publisher: Card No. 121951, Tichcorner Quality Views.
Manufacturer: Not Indicated.

North Side Senior High School, Corning, N. Y.

117949-N

The cornerstone for the Northside Senior High School was laid in 1926. The school was built on land that was originally part of the Kingsbury Plot. The building was designed by Mr. Palmer Rodgers and constructed by the Corning Building Company. It included an auditorium, a gymnasium, a model house for the study of home economics and a telephone in every classroom. The school is currently known as the Northside-Blodget Junior High School and is located on Princeton Avenue.

Publisher: Card No. 117949-N, Lamb's Pharmacy, Corning, NY.
Manufacturer: Curteich, Chicago, IL.

D. L. & W. Passenger Station, Corning, N. Y.

In the 1880's Corning's busy railroad industry received a new competitor. The Delaware, Lackawanna, and Western Railroad began a route through Gibson to the Northside of Corning. The first railroad station for the DL&W was located in Gibson with the passengers traveling by coach for the long trip to Corning. In 1902, the DL&W moved the station from Gibson to the head of Bridge Street in the Northside of Corning.

Publisher: Not Indicated.
Manufacturer: Not Indicated.

The concept of bringing coal by railroad from Pennsylvania to the area that is now Corning and the Feeder Canal was a large step toward the beginning of Corning. The railroad line that accomplished this movement of coal grew into the Fall Brook Railroad Company. It later became the Pennsylvania Division of the New York Central Railroad. The New York Central Railyards in North Corning were a showcase for the Eastern Railroad Industry. These two photographs show different sections of these busy Railyards.

Publisher: Hugh C. Lighten Company, Portland, ME.
Manufacturer: Frankfurt, Germany.

Publisher: Card no. 219048, Not Indicated.
Manufacturer: Not Indicated.

The Imperial Club was located in Riverside. Over the years the building had various names including, *"The Brick House", "The Goffe House," "Elmwood", "YMCA Building",* and the *"Imperial Club".* The construction was between 1850 and 1852 by Mr. William Erwin. Their were many owners until 1913 when it was purchased by the Ingersoll-Rand Company. The building was renovated and a dormitory wing was added to provide a place for visitors and employees of the company. In 1971, the building was given to the YMCA as a local center of activity. A fire in 1972 caused extensive damage and the YMCA was forced to abandon the building be-

IMPERIAL CLUB, PAINTED POST, N. Y.

cause of the high cost of repairs. Another fire completely destroyed the building in the early 1980's.

Publisher: Not Indicated.
Manufacturer: Not Indicated.

HODGMAN'S MILL, PAINTED POST, N.Y.

The original building, on the left, was built on West Water Street by Captain Samuel Erwin as a flour mill in 1823. A saw mill, powered by undershot water wheels, was added to the rear of the building. A few years later a shingle and plaster mill was added. This photograph was taken in 1937. Mr. Lyman Hodgman was the last owner of the property and after his death it was acquired by Ingersoll-Rand. After 1940, the site was used as a parking lot. Today, Hodgman Park occupies most of this area.

Publisher: Not Indicated.
Manufacturer: Not Indicated.

I.O.O.F. Temple Painted Post, N.Y.

The International Organization of Odd Fellows Temple was established in 1910. Their Temple is shown in the background. Today, the old iron bridge shown in the center of the photograph is no longer a part of this scene.

Publisher: Not Indicated.
Manufacturer: Not Indicated.

Painted Post Indian Monument, Corning, N. Y.

A cast monument of the legendary John Montour, created in 1894, placed on a 15-foot stone pedestal at the intersection of High and Hamilton Streets. In 1934, the monument was moved to Traffic Island and in 1948 a windstorm toppled the monument and it was shattered. On May 30, 1950, a new Indian made of bronze, was placed at the original site. The design was by Mr. Norman Phelps, a local art teacher. After the Agnes Flood in 1972, the monument was moved to the Village Square Park, on the corner of High and Hamilton Streets. The monument was intended to signify Painted Post as a place marked by a Painted Indian Post.

Publisher: Not Indicated.
Manufacturer: Not Indicated.

Looking North at the corner of Hamilton and High Streets we see dirt streets and various buildings. On the left is the Bronson Block begun in 1861 including two stores and a public hall. On the right corner was the Terbell Drug Store. In the rear of the photograph, behind the Indian Monument, is the Fish Block built in the 1870's. The third floor was added to the building after 1886. On the same side of the street as the Fish Block was the Masonic Hall built in 1870 with a front facade of all cast iron. Also, an interesting use of sheet iron is the small figure of an Indian, erected circa 1880. The figure is on a pole, located to the right of the telephone pole, at the right side of the

Business Square and Indian Monument, Painted Post, N.Y.

photograph. Note the little boy pulling his red(?) wagon and the sign on the wall of the building extolling *"Paines Celery Compound."*

Publisher: Not Indicated.
Manufacturer: Not Indicated.

Ingersoll Rand Plant, Painted Post, N. Y.

The Ingersoll-Rand plant began during the Post Civil War Industrialization period. Its function had been to repair machinery for the mills located along the river. Mr. Simon Ingersoll, an inventor and mechanic, developed a power rock drill which was improved by Mr. Henry C. Sargant, and financed by Mr. John Minor. In 1887, The Ingersoll-Sargant Drill Company, Phillipsburg, New Jersey, and the Rand Drill Company moved to New York State. This merger, in 1905, combined two experienced and successful makers of drills. A merger in 1987, changed the company name to Dresser-Rand Company.

Publisher: Not Indicated.
Manufacturer: Not Indicated.

Presbyterian Church and Manse, Painted Post, N.Y.

The Presbyterian Church was incorporated in 1839 and the building was constructed on Hamilton Street for $5,200 in 1883. The dirt road shown in the photograph shows the street car tracks coming from Corning and crossing railroad tracks. During the Agnes flood in 1972, the water damaged the church to the extent that it was razed and a new church was constructed. The new church is shared with a Methodist Congregation.

Publisher: Baker Bros., Elmira, NY.
Manufacturer: Made In Germany.

Methodist Church, Painted Post, N.Y.

The Methodists of Painted Post held their first meeting in a room over a store. They built their first church in 1850. The church shown in this photograph was constructed in 1928 and was razed after the flood in 1972.

Publisher: Not Indicated.
Manufacturer: Not Indicated.

Charles St., Painted Post, N. Y.

Looking North from the corner of Charles and West Water Streets. The home, as shown in the photograph, was built circa 1890 by the Castle Family. The people and the land in this area were important to Painted Post becoming a key location on the Andaste Trail. The trail was used by the indians, early settlers, and land speculators who often met at Painted Post. The name came from a painted wooden indian post located at the center of the village. Early settlers created a sheet metal Indian monument in 1824. In 1894, a cast iron figure was erected.

Publisher: Not Indicated.
Manufacturer: Not Indicated.

NEW ERIE DEPOT.

The Erie Railroad was one of the most important factors in the growth of Painted Post. The constant improvements to the railroad helped to sustain the business growth. The new Erie Station, circa 1930, was one of the improvements that helped to increase the services provide by the railroad.

Publisher: Not Indicated.
Manufacturer: Not indicated.

Mill Street, Savona, N. Y.

5060-PHOTOGRAPHED AND PUBLISHED BY THOS. B. JAMISON.

Water power was a very important factor in the growth of Savona. Based on this growth potential the early businesses included:

A Grist Mill owned by Mr. George Allen.

A Planing Mill owned by Mr. Clarence Hubbard.

The Patent Sluice factory of Mr. Charles Davis.

Two General Stores.

Two Drug Stores.

One Furniture and Undertaking Establishment.

One Jewelry Store.

Two Hotels.

Three Blacksmiths.

A Carriage Shop.

A Cigar Factory.

A Music Store

A Meat Market

A Barber Shop.

Two Milliners.

One Newspaper— *"Savona Review"*.

Publisher: Card No. 5060, Thomas B. Jamison.
Manufacturer: N. E. Paper & Stationary Company, Ayer, MA.

Looking down the River from Mill St. Bridge, Savona, N. Y.

5059-PHOTOGRAPHED AND PUBLISHED BY THOS. B. JAMISON

A stream called Mud Creek discharged into the Conhocton River at the village site. In the early history of Savona, this junction of the two sources of water was important to the lumbermen and boatmen on both bodies of water. As a result, this source of water contributed to the growth of the village. The railroads later took over much of the business activity that initially traveled by water.

Publisher: Card No. 5059, Thomas B. Jamison.
Manufacturer: N. E. Paper & Stationary Company, Ayer, MA.

Looking North from Main Street, Savona, N. Y.

5033-PHOTOGRAPHED & PUBLISHED BY THOS. B JAMISON

The Village of Savona was incorporated in 1883 and later annexed to Bath. The early community included a Post Office and a Trading Center established circa 1823. A Union School District was organized in 1891. This photograph shows how early settlers had the advantage of the forest-covered hills and waterways. As a result, lumber mills were built on Mud Creek. The lumber products were floated to Baltimore, Maryland by way of the Chemung and Susquehanna Rivers.

Publisher: Card No. 5033, Thomas B. Jamison.
Manufacturer: N.E. Paper & Stationary Company, Ayer, MA.

B1881H20   **Fish Hatchery, Bath, N. Y.**
Pub. by Chas. E. Buck, Music House.

The Fish Hatchery is located approximately three miles from Bath on the Old Bath-Hammondsport Road. The Hatchery is on fifteen acres of the most beautiful land in the County. The property includes the Cold Brook Stream with the purest water found anywhere in the U.S.A. The water, emanates from the West of the Hatchery, beginning in innumerable little underground springs all providing an abundant supply of cold water for the fish ponds. This water does not vary more than four degrees in temperature from February to August. This constant temperature was the reason the State selected to build the original Hatchery buildings on this site in 1894.

Publisher: Card No. B1881H20, Chas. E. Buck, Music House.
Manufacturer: Not Indicated.

Pultney Park.   BATH, N. Y.

Pulteney Park had a beginning when in 1794, one hundred yards up from a river landing, a Colonel Williamson plotted out a central opening and named it Pulteney Square. He put Mr. Henry McElwee to work chopping down trees *"Carefully and close to the ground."* A single pine tree was left standing in front of the Agency House as a Liberty Tree. It was trimmed leaving a small tuft on the top. The tree remained as a lonely sentinel until 1820 when it was toppled during a windstorm.

Publisher: Not Indicated.
Manufacturer: Not Indicated.

The New York State Soldiers' and Sailors' Home was built on the Rider Farm which included 241 acres of land approximately 1-½ miles northwest of Bath. The architects were Warner and Cutler of Rochester, New York. The cornerstone was laid on June 13, 1877 and the Reverend Henry Ward Beecher spoke at the ceremony. The foundations for the three buildings were made of stone taken from a quarry on the farm. The first officers at the home were Mr. E. C. Parkinson, Superintendent; Mr. Daniel O'Driscoll, Post-Adjutant; and Secretary, Mr. A. H. Nash. These men were all veterans of the Civil War and well qualified by experience to be in charge of this institution.

Company B.   N. Y. State Soldiers' and Sailors' Home.   BATH, N. Y.
Company C.
Companies D, E & F.

Publisher: Samuel N. Harper.
Manufacturer: Not Indicated.

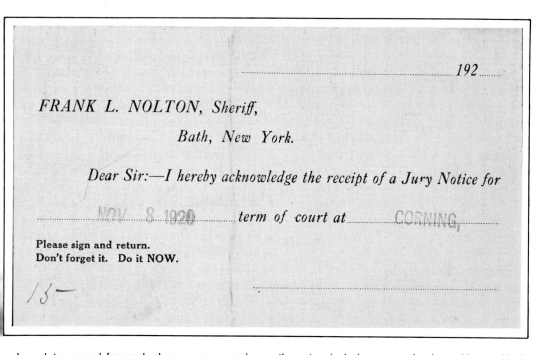

.... *192*......

FRANK L. NOLTON, Sheriff,

Bath, New York.

Dear Sir:—I hereby acknowledge the receipt of a Jury Notice for

...........NOV 8 1920............ *term of court at*............CORNING,............

Please sign and return.
Don't forget it. Do it NOW.

Jury duty moved forward when women made another step in being recognized as citizens. Until 1937, Steuben County juries were made up of "*Good Men and True*", but never women. During July 1937, the first list of women was drawn for jury duty. They were selected on the same basis as men: citizen, 21 to 70 years of age, in good health and of good character, and owner of realty assessed at $150 or more, or the husband (or wife) of such an owner.

Publisher: Not Indicated.
Manufacturer: Not Indicated.

CURTISS AEROPLANE FACTORY AND AVIATION GROUNDS, HAMMONDSPORT, N, Y.

Among the events that Hammondsport can indicate with pride is the work of Glenn H. Curtiss. He built and tested his early airplanes, from 1907—1912, in the buildings located near the edge of the water (As shown in the left center of the upper photograph).

In July 1908, Mr. Curtiss made history by flying his "June Bug" for more than one mile creating a new distance record for flight. The lower photograph shows Mr. Curtiss testing the controls of the June Bug prior to another flight. His ground crew, standing to his right and left, are helping him to make the required adjustments in the controls.

Publisher: Card No. A-56793, C.T. American Art.
Manufacturer: Not Indicated.

G. H. CURTISS READY FOR THE START IN HIS AEROPLANE, "JUNE BUG,"
HAMMONDSPORT, N. Y.

Publisher: Not Indicated.
Manufacturer: Not Indicated.

This stately home located on a large estate known as the Aisle of Pines, near Wayne in the Town of Tyrone, was built approximately at the time when the Civil War started. The home was the dream of Mr. Samuel Hallet, a banker and investor. He was shot by an unknown assassin in 1864. The second owner was Mr. George K. Birge, a businessman from Buffalo, New York, who had turned his Birge Bicycle Company into the Pierce Arrow Motor Car Company. He enlarged the home, built a swimming pool nearby, and moved the house to turn it away from Waneta Lake to face Keuka Lake. Various other owners have had the home. During the unoccupied periods it was seriously vandalized, burglarized, and bonfires were started on its hardwood floors. During the last of these periods, the home was destroyed by fire.

Publisher: Not Indicated.
Manufacturer: Not Indicated.

BIBLIOGRAPHY

The following books and publications were used as sources of information in preparing this book:

Allen, Fred E.,   HANDBOOK OF THE N.Y.S. REFORMATORY AT ELMIRA., Summary, 1916

Byrne, Thomas E.,   CHEMUNG COUNTY 1890-1975, Chemung County Historical Association., 1976.

Clayton, W.W.,   HISTORY OF STEUBEN COUNTY NEW YORK., Lewis, 1879.

Chemung County   ELMIRA CENTENNIAL 1864-1964., Commercial Press, 1964.
Historical Society

Dimitroff, Thomas P.   HISTORY OF THE CORNING—PAINTED POST AREA: 200 YEARS IN PAINTED POST
& Louis S. Janes   COUNTRY., Corning Area Bicentennial Committee, 1977.

Elmira Advertising   ELMIRA PAST & PRESENT: ITS COMMERCE, TRADE, & INDUSTRIES., Elmira Advertising
Association   Assocation., 1894.

Hakes, Harlo, Editor,   LANDMARKS OF STEUBEN COUNTY, NEW YORK., Mason, 1896.

Malone, Harry R.,   ONE HUNDRED & FIFTY YEARS OF PROGRESS., 1929.

McNamara, Robert F.,   A CENTURY OF GRACE: THE HISTORY OF ST. MARY'S ROMAN CATHOLIC PARISH,
                                            CORNING, NEW YORK 1848-1948., St. Mary's Church, 1979.

Mulford, Uri,   PIONEER DAYS & LATER TIMES IN CORNING AND VICINITY 1789-1920., Uri Mulford.

Near, Irwin W.,   A HISTORY OF STEUBEN COUNTY., NEW YORK, 2 Volumes, Lewis, 1911.

Near Westside   THE HISTORIC NEAR WESTSIDE: ELMIRA, NEW YORK., 1981.
Neighborhood Association

Page, N.R.,   ELMIRA ILLUSTRATED., Part Two of Nine Parts, N. R. Page & Company, 1890.

Pierce, Henry B.,   HISTORY OF TIOGA, CHEMUNG, TOMPKINS, AND SCHUYLER COUNTIES, NEW YORK.,
                                            Everts and Ensign, 1879.

Reed, Roger G.,   ARCHITECTS OF STANDING: PIERCE & BICKFORD ELMIRA NEW YORK., 1890-1932,
                                            Chemung County Historical Society, 1983.

Roberts, Millard F., Editor,   HISTORICAL GAZETTEER OF STEUBEN COUNTY NEW YORK WITH MEMOIRS AND
                                            ILLUSTRATIONS, 1891.

Taylor, Eva,   A SHORT HISTORY OF ELMIRA., Steele Memorial Library, 1937

Thrall, W.B., Editor,   PIONEER HISTORY AND ATLAS OF STEUBEN COUNTY, NEW YORK., W.B. Thrall, 1942.

Towner, Ausburn,   OUR COUNTY AND ITS PEOPLE; A HISTORY OF THE VALLEY AND THE COUNTY OF
                                            CHEMUNG., D. Mason, 1892.